Transformation and Emerging Markets

Transformation and Emerging Markets

George Macesich

Westport, Connecticut
London

Library of Congress Cataloging-in-Publication Data

Macesich, George, 1927–
    Transformation and emerging markets / George Macesich.
      p.   cm.
    Includes bibliographical references and index.
    ISBN 0–275–95518–4 (alk. paper)
    1. International economic relations. 2. International economic
integration. 3. Investments, Foreign. 4. International trade.
5. National state. I. Title.
HF1359.M33   1996
337—dc20   96–16273

British Library Cataloguing in Publication Data is available.

Library of Congress Catalog Card Number: 96–16273
ISBN: 0–275–95518–4

First published in 1996

Praeger Publishers, 88 Post Road West, Westport, CT 06881
An imprint of Greenwood Publishing Group, Inc.

Printed in the United States of America

The paper used in this book complies with the
Permanent Paper Standard issued by the National
Information Standards Organization (Z39.48–1984).

10 9 8 7 6 5 4 3 2 1

For
Dragomir Vojnić
Scholar, Colleague, and Friend

Contents

Preface

This study argues that the economics and history of the closing years of the 20th century may turn out to be called the era of transformation. Nation-states have lost most of their room for maneuver in the transnationalization of finance and investment that now affects them all. In the European Community and in future imitations of that association elsewhere, nation-states will also lose some formal powers. The most effective of European social democracies have had to modify their policies, and in Scandinavia have been voted out of power. An economically sustainable social democracy may be beyond the reach of any one nation-state. In fact, many analysts conclude that any political and economic reforms which take only the nation-state as a starting point are doomed. The question, then, is how to square the transnational economy with national identity and the nation-state. Increasingly, the responsibilities of the nation-state have to be transferred to more powerful world entities. It may be that middle-sized nation-states of the kind that exist in Europe and elsewhere are too small to deal with large problems and too large to deal with the small ones.

Two developments, moreover, have served to reinforce the growing movement to integrate world markets. One, of course, is the fall of communism. The other is the ability and willingness of businesses to internationalize their activities to maximize profits and minimize costs.

I would like to express appreciation to Dr. Carol Bullock for assistance in completing this study.

Transformation and Emerging Markets

1

Era of Transformation:
In Search of a Role Model

AN END TO NATIONALISTIC FINANCE AND INVESTMENT?

History of the closing years of the 20th century may turn out to be called the era of transformation. Nation-states have lost most of their room for maneuver in the transnationalization of finance and investment that now affects them all. In the European Community, and in future imitations of that association elsewhere, nation-states will also lose some formal powers. The most effective European social democracies have had to modify their policies, and in Scandinavia have been voted out of power. An economically sustainable social democracy may be beyond the reach of any one nation-state. In fact, many analysts conclude that any political and economic reforms that take the nation-state as a starting and end point are doomed.

In essence, the question is how to square the transnational economy with national identity and the nation-state. Increasingly, the responsibilities of the nation-state have to be transferred to more powerful entities. It may be that middle-sized nation-states of the kind that exist in Europe and elsewhere are too small to deal with large problems and too large to deal with the small ones. Some politicians have long seen this. For Jean Monet in Paris in the 1940s, as for liberals and socialists and old conservatives in Germany, Greece, Spain, and Portugal somewhat later, a European Union was the best insurance for the future against the past. Nationalism has to be drained out of politics. It may be that the last best hope for a country's national politics is that it cease to be a national politics.

Certainly, it is unlikely (as Marxists used to hope) that transnationalized capitalism and nationalism will disappear together. Nor is it likely, as some used to believe, that the second will outlive the first. Quite the opposite. It is now more generally wondered whether transnationalized capitalism is not final and nation-states are fated to become nominal. These observers may be right even though nationalism continues undiminished.

It is little surprise that nation-states and their governments still matter in the world of finance and investment. Thus their policies still exert strong influences, and their bonds, equities, and investment and saving instruments are traded around the world. Mexico, for instance, got into trouble in 1994–1995 because its government tried to influence domestic elections by printing money while at the same time attempting to maintain a fixed exchange rate for its peso. Money market managers in world markets simply refused to go along with the Mexican government's inflationary program and dumped Mexican securities with predict-able results. The entire Mexican episode is but another illustration of the tight linkage between global markets.

In a world where money flows back and forth across borders, a nation's leadership may put on the sociopolitical and socioeconomic show, but it is the international money managers who write the reviews and the country's citizens that reap the consequences. Thus it is that when American interest rates increased in 1994, a lot of "hot money" that had been flowing to emerging markets such as Mexico moved back into the better known American market. One consequence, of course, was that the emerging markets sagged and some investors lost money. It is also true, unfortunately, that with emerging markets opening up in China, former the Soviet Union, and Eastern Europe, many people have been making investments in unfamiliar places and in financial instruments they do not understand, with predictable results.

The sad fact is that when a country's government dies, its people must pay, and very soon. The recent Mexican fiasco is but a case in point. Without either a vote or debate in either the United States or in Mexico, the U.S. government de facto took over Mexico's economic future. Many observers have judged this decision as not only the result of mismanagement but of falsehoods, evasions, and self-delusions by the Mexican and U.S. governments.[1] In 1994 the two governments attempted to convince Americans that Mexico was strong enough financially and politically to enter an economic partnership with the United States in the form of the North American Free Trade Agreement (NAFTA) and that workers and investors in both countries would benefit.

By the second half of 1994, as the Mexican economy tumbled into serious troubles, officials in both countries kept silent. As the Mexican peso collapsed in December 1994, it became clear that Mexico was about to default—a fact well known to officials in both countries much earlier.

By early 1995, the American government stepped forth with a multibillion-dollar program to prevent Mexico from going into bankruptcy. Mexican and U.S. investors may have been saved by the multibillion-dollar rescue plan; the plan may also have saved Mexican politicians who, according to Senator Daniel Patrick Moynihan, have been running a one-party Leninist system. For most Mexicans, the thought of becoming wards of the United States and surrendering their oil as collateral may not sit well. If they repudiate the whole arrangement or revolt, what options does the American government have?

Certainly, the results of March 1995 are not encouraging. Mexico's foreign bond holders are cashing in their bonds for pesos as soon as they reach maturity, and then they are taking those pesos to Mexican banks, changing them into dollars, and taking them back north. The banks are getting the dollars to pay the foreigners from the Mexican government, and the Mexican government is getting the dollars on loan from the U.S. Treasury. In effect, the peso is simply being dumped instead of stabilized, which would invite investment.

In the absence of a believable program for the economic and political transformation of Mexico, the lack of domestic and foreign confidence in the country and its government is understandable. The conspiratorial shadows swirling around Mexico's political and economic elite do no help matters. The United States has political capital invested in Mexico—one reason, perhaps, that decent notice was not given of a coming disaster. According to some observers, matters were not helped by the fact that many analysts have become part of a broad marketing, underwriting, and distribution network in securities that may have compromised their objectivity.

South Africa is another country in the processes of painful transformation. Of the country's many problems, most are related to the redistribution of wealth. By most accounts, President Nelson Mandela was shocked, upon emerging from prison, to discover that the world's socialists had become free marketeers. He forced his party, the African National Congress, to abandon its long-standing promise to nationalize South Africa's industries. The nation's white business leadership are among President Mandela's strongest supporters and contributors.

President Mandela has a serious transformation problem to resolve: how to have a stable and productive economy presided over by corporations that enjoy international confidence and political stability, which are almost certainly tied to the black masses' expectations of a speedy redistribution of income. It is generally agreed that a new biracial wage-earning middle class is needed; less agreement exists on whether the white business leadership will move quickly enough to head off political upheaval. The central issue in the transformation of South Africa is how to proceed in the sensitive work of building a new structure for economic justice and representative government that is fair to the governing black majority and the new white minority.

President Mandela's task is not made easier by the behavior of his estranged wife, Winnie Mandela. Her regal style of militancy has made her the favorite of South Africa's dispossessed: the squatter communities, rural poor, and township youth. Many people note that she gives voice to widespread frustration with the slowness of the transformation processes and with the perception that the government is more interested in appeasing whites in the name of reconciliation than in addressing the needs of the black majority.

Winnie Mandela's weakness may be that, like all populist icons, her support base is wobbly because she relies on visceral appeal, not on organizational strength. Nevertheless, as long as the government is perceived as failing to begin delivering its promises of jobs, education, housing, and justice to the people who put it in power, a demagogic takeover of political power is possible.

Transformation issues are also clearly in the forefront of discussions regarding the future of the European Union (EU). Germany continues to press Great Britain to accept greater powers in the European parliament and an extension of majority voting for EU governments' decision making. Germany argues that the EU can become a more cohesive force in political and economic decision making only if individual states gave up their national veto. At present, majority voting is largely limited to questions concerning the single market.

For its part, France is confronting an open secret that the nation's business and political elite had intimate and mutually beneficial ties—far more blatant ones than in other countries. French industrial giants channeled campaign contributions through off-shore accounts, and in between their exports were promoted by government officials. Within France they were given captive markets, and any bribes were considered a necessary cost of doing business. French politicians and chief executives alike were kept mostly beyond the reach of the criminal courts.

Now that government-controlled companies are being privatized and thrown into a global competitive economy, the former cozy relationship has been shaken. The processes of transformation in France may be seen as a struggle between idealism and power and as Anglo-Saxon values being imposed on Gallic corporate government. The fact is that transformation is taking hold in France. Similar processes were underway in Italy at the end of the 1980s (and continue into the 1990s), and took the form of dealing with the corrupt aspects of large industrial groups.

It is interesting to note the rather prominent role the political left in Italy is playing in the country's social, political, and economic transformation. For the Italian communists, influence with the country's electorate began roughly in the 1980s and early 1990s, when they presumably renounced Marxism and adapted a less threatening name, the Party of the Democratic Left. Ever since the formation of the Italian Republic following World War II, the Communists directed their energies principally into hundreds of local administrations and the labor movement, due in good part to their inability to move into the executive branch of government.

In both the local administration and the labor movement, the communists were generally respected for their efficiency, sense of innovation, and probity. In fact, the Party of the Democratic Left was the only major party not affected by the Italian corruption scandals of the 1980s and early 1990s. The amalgamation in the 1980s of the three major labor unions was largely spearheaded by the communist labor union. In its expanded, coordinated form, the labor movement has gained considerable support from its membership and has increased its impact on management.

In fact, the Party of the Democratic Left supported the interim government of technocrats of Prime Minister Lamberto Dini with its March 16, 1995, vote of confidence. Thus, in a sense, the Party ratified the austerity programs Dini had proposed to restore financial stability to Italy. By casting more than 50 percent of the yes vote, the Party became the decisive political factor in extending and expanding the tenure of the Dini government.

Even Japan had made some modest moves toward reducing regulations impeding the free flow of trade. In early 1995, the Japanese government disclosed a five-year program to abolish or relax hundreds of economic regulations. The package includes a wide range of industries. Some of the rule changes should make it less expensive to import goods and transport them in Japan, while other rules might ease the use of American wood products in Japanese homes. Other rules would not be changed or revised but only reviewed. Many of the 1,100 items are steps that had already been announced. The plan leaves out deregulatory steps proposed by both Japanese industry and foreign businesses.

Deregulation has become a significant issue in the early 1990s. Analysts argue that it would bring down high prices and revitalize the world economy by easing new business formulation. The United States and Europe have pressed for deregulation to ease the entry of foreign companies into Japanese markets. In fact, some business interests in Japan charge that a strong deregulatory effort would eventually help reduce Japan's trade surplus and so help stem the rapid rise of the yen against the dollar. These charges stand little chance of realization. Thus the plan includes only 211 of the 456 deregulatory measures recommended by Japan's leading business organizations.

Japan has introduced numerous deregulation and input-promotion packages over the years. But when put into effect, the plans usually fall short. For instance, the most recent plan leaves decisions on what rules to eliminate to the bureaucrats who have a vested interest in maintaining the rules. On the positive side, the most recent plan at least provides for annual reviews open to foreign suggestions and sets more specific time tables than in the past.

Is fairness to critics of American exporters to Japan it should be pointed out that the American government cannot go to Tokyo and compel the Japanese to buy American products and services. For instance, it is ridiculous to complain that the Japanese do not buy cars from America's Big Three automobile producers. These producers did not produce right-hand-driving cars until 1993. To this day, the American automobile press consistently rates most Japanese-brand cars above most American-brand automobiles within a given price range. Demanding that the Japanese buy more American cars would be akin to the former East Germans requiring Americans to buy right-hand-driving Trabauts. Such a request, of course, would be met with skepticism in the United States.

There is little doubt that critics have a point that unless the United States and, for that matter, Europe start producing products that Japanese consumers want to buy and market such products in a way the Japanese find attractive, both Americans and Europeans will keep failing. No amount of weight throwing by them will propel the individual Japanese citizen to buy their products. Can we sincerely imagine the individual European or American jumping to buy more from another country simply because the country in question—say Brazil—demands that its trade imbalance be reduced?

Japan has one of the most managed economies in the world, and the only way into that economy is to be managed in. Trade barriers are deeply rooted in Japanese society, and it will take more than continuing appreciation of the yen to open the Japanese market. One approach that has not brought about the desired results is a broad-based framework approach to negotiation. Apparently, the approach was too broad based. Discussions deteriorated into endless discussions about what constitutes open trade.

The collapse of the Soviet Union and other socialist countries in east and central Europe has confronted policy makers and others with serious problems. Clearly, the conversion of the formerly socialist countries of Europe to market democracy and/or some variation will not be a simple task. The many social, economic, and political problems assure that it will be a formidable task. The industrial structures in these countries are obsolete by virtually any standard of measure. They were constructed not on a division of labor based on a country's comparative advantage, but rather to meet the needs of government plans. These plans in turn aimed at making the country nearly as self-sufficient as possible. One consequence of such policies is that government strongly supported inefficient industries. The net result is that now the production system in these countries must be modernized and adjusted to the requirements of international standards. Similarly, the domestic infrastructure required to facilitate and support such standards must be modernized.

Even more important, moreover, are the requirements made on a country's human resources. Clearly more investment in the human agent, including education and health, is required. A number of these countries are removed by a generation or more from experience with market economies and the entrepreneurial and managerial expertise needed to make such economies function properly.

These problems are further compounded by the pace at which the transformation is to take. Much has been said in favor of the so-called big bang, which means the reforms needed are implemented immediately. In effect, prices (including exchange rates) are freed from state control and allowed to find their free market rates. These measures envision the elimination of subsidies of economic activity. A major concern with the big bank approach to transformation is that unemployment may rise to socially unacceptable levels, as may as prices for many essential goods and services.

An alternative approach is to adopt a gradual approach whereby the necessary changes are spaced over time to minimize the consequences of inflation and unemployment. The idea is to implement and consolidate one reform measure before going on to the next. One problem with such an approach is that market economies do not function efficiently and effectively when some prices are free while others remain controlled. Such an arrangement encourages the production of goods and services whose prices are not under control. Another problem is that many necessary reforms will not be implemented.

A FREE MARKET AS A ROLE MODEL?

Certainly, time has not come to an end. A new world order consisting of market democracies, liberal democratic ideals, and free market economies has yet to arrive. In fact, history is far from over. We may expect that the new wave of world integration will lead to new opportunities and adjustments.[2]

Countries have in place various versions of market economies. Some of them draw more than others on elements and components of market democracy. Others may be at various stages on the path to market democracy. Some of them may be on different paths to such democracy that are more in tune with their own historic and social circumstances—all the more reason that if world markets are to become integrated with a minimum of world friction and conflict, it is imperative that countries with diverse systems be enabled to participate in the processes and benefits of integration.

I have suggested elsewhere that a regime of truly flexible exchange rates (and not the "dirty" float version of such a regime) would promote the world's fourth wave of integration underway in the post-cold war period.[3] Such a regime can serve to promote the uniqueness, diversity, and sovereignty of world nations. It is a regime, moreover, consistent with market democracy. Furthermore, it does not depend for success on the constant hectoring by major world powers; nor, for that matter, does it depend on a busybody world bureaucracy.

It is not surprising that the European Union under existing exchange rate arrangements has spent most of the period since the fall of the Berlin Wall in 1989 trying to strengthen links among West European members instead of reaching out to the postcommunist countries of the East, unnecessarily complicating Easterners' transition to market democracy. This is what Professor Milton Friedman suggested years ago would likely be the case in the absence of a regime of flexible rates in the European Community. Free markets and exchange rates are more likely to be successful in promoting economic integration than a bureaucracy.

Clearly, economic integration is as important to East European stability as, say, NATO membership, and far less provocative to Moscow. The dissimilarity in economic arrangements existing in Eastern Europe (and, for that matter, elsewhere in the world) and the remainder of Europe can be better accommodated within a system of flexible exchange rates. The expensive acquisition of East Germany into West Germany under a regime of a more or less fixed exchange rate has been shown to be a very expensive venture indeed. Other East European countries do not have a West German benefactor, even though West Germany appears to be the main champion of bringing in the East. Certainly, Germany has a strong interest in the viability of its eastern neighbors since that viability affects its own national security. Germans do not relish the idea that their eastern boundary may become the frontier between a "have" and "have not" Europe. There is also good reason to assume that Great Britain favors eastward expansion for the political and economic opportunities such expansion may provide.

Not everyone favors a German-oriented east. In particular, the Mediterranean countries—France, Italy, Greece, Portugal, and Spain—are less than enthusiastic about the opening toward the east. No doubt the concerns of these countries turn on the possibility of a reallocation in regional subsidies, competition for their favors and a shift in the European Union's political center from the Mediterranean toward the German-oriented east. To this concern may also be added the possibility of neglect of the Mediterranean countries' own security concerns about Islamic militants in nearby North Africa.

The extent to which the United States will participate in binding together a long-divided continent is an open question. The U.S. tilt toward Germany in the post-cold war period and the Yugoslav catastrophe does not help reassure Mediterranean countries that German influence will not be dominant and their concerns over North Africa and Islam marginalized. Matters are not calmed on this score by the American tilt toward Turkey in spite of that country's sordid human rights record. A more even-handed approach by the United States would probably reassure these countries that their concerns would not be slighted.

Adam Smith states more than 200 years ago that the "invisible hand" of the free market produces many beneficial economic results. It may also produce certain beneficial political efforts. Certainly, changes in the global economy, which in good measure stem from integration of the world's economy, have also produced desirable political results. The collapse of the Soviet Union was a result of millions of people demanding free markets and participation in the world economy. The impact of the collapse continues to reverberate throughout the world.

It is not clear that if the European Union attempts to press its will on an increasingly diverse constituency, people and nations will fare better. Obviously, the idea is to find the right balance between the unique and personal identity of nations and the opportunities and demands of a larger entity whether the European Union and/or global economy. Yugoslavia and the Soviet Union are but examples where such a balance was not struck. The future may indeed hold other examples.

NOTES

1. See, for instance, A.M. Rosenthal, "Taking Over Mexico," *New York Times*, February 24, 1995. p. A15.

2. See George Macesich, *Integration and Stability: A Monetary View* (Westport, CT: Greenwood Press, 1995).

3. Ibid.

2

Economics and Politics
of Emerging Markets

INTEGRATING WORLD FINANCIAL MARKETS

Attempts at strengthening and accelerating what I have described elsewhere as the fourth wave of world integration can be seen in the sphere of international money and finance and, in particular, in the world's capital markets.[1] Felix Rohatyn puts it well: Despite threats and conflicts within different regions of the world, growth of worldwide capital markets has gone ahead relentlessly. A legitimate worldwide market in stocks, bonds, currencies, and other financial instruments has emerged, tied together by modern data processing and communications technology and operating twenty-four hours a day. It is variously estimated that between 1990 and 2020, the output of the G-7 "rich countries" will grow from $13 trillion to $24 trillion, for an average growth rate of less than 2 percent per year. The output of the "nonrich" or "emerging market" countries (e.g., China, India, Indonesia, Russia) is expected to grow from $9 trillion to $34 trillion over the same period, or about 4.5 percent per year.

Assuming, for the sake of argument, that these estimates are reasonable, larger amounts of capital will be required to sustain such growth. Global competition for capital will likely concentrate the attention of countries in need of capital on making economic and political reforms likely to encourage the mobilization of domestic and foreign savings. If they are to tap into private investment, these countries must push ahead with reforms aimed at a stable currency, receptive social and political institutions, and, of course, a growing economy.

Given the magnitude and risks involved, it is with good reason that Rohatyn suggests the adoption of worldwide investment standards. He argues that there should be a separate and comprehensive organization comparable to the General Agreement on Tariffs and Trade (GATT) for investment, just as there is a GATT for trade, even though some aspects of investment are covered under GATT. If such arrangements are in place, it is likely that Western investors, including pension funds, insurance funds, mutual funds, and others with fiduciary responsibilities, will look with added interest into foreign investment.

Other countries also fall far short of guaranteeing international investors the kinds of protection now given by American securities legislation. For instance, the European Community has made attempts in this direction and encourages regulation to protect investors. How far such efforts have to go is suggested by the case of Germany, where only in 1994 was legislation introduced requiring higher disclosure standards, more adequate protection for minority shareholders, and severe penalties for insider trading. In fact, in 1994 Daimler-Benz was the only major German company to adopt the accounting standards that have been a basic requirement of American securities laws for years if a firm is to be listed on the New York Stock Exchange.

It is thus with good reason that an appropriate model may be the features of the American capital market. The legal protections; the requirement of disclosure; the variety of financial instruments available to investors, including stocks, bonds, mutual funds, options, and futures; the technical capacities of the system—all suggest standards lacking in many countries. They will, however, be required if local capital markets are to be connected in a satisfactory manner will global markets. In any case, the capital necessary to finance reasonable rates of growth worldwide is beyond the capacities of the West, either from public or private funds. Efficient and effective capital markets in all countries are necessary to provide for and sustain the fourth wave of international integration.

ROCKY ROAD FOR EMERGING MARKETS

The problems in Mexico in 1994–1995 that have led to a devaluation of the Mexican peso have cast emerging markets in a new light. Ripples from that crisis spread not only to other Latin American countries, but also to emerging markets around the world.

Mutual funds, one of the more popular investment vehicles for investing in emerging markets, suggest that Latin American funds led the list of losers in early 1995, with declines of 30 percent. Foreign funds fell an average of 3 percent. American investors have responded to the gloomy picture by keeping money close to home. Thus net new sales of international funds sank to $445 million in February 1995, a tenth of the level of a year earlier, according to the Investment Company Institute, a mutual fund association.

Financial planners routinely recommend some foreign investments to reduce the volatility in portfolios because stock markets do not move in tandem. Moreover, many foreign economies have higher rates of return than that of the United States, suggesting more potential for appreciation. Mexico in 1995 had few defenders in the fraternity of financial analysts. Europe, however, had many proponents. Even some emerging markets were favored by analysts. Such emerging markets as Peru, Poland, and the Philippines catch the favorable attention of analysts. Funds that invest in Pacific Rim countries in general were down an average of almost 4 percent in early 1995. Moreover, foreign funds that invested in stocks of small companies abroad suffered the most in the same period.

As in every venture, the potential investor in emerging markets should be alert to problems. Thus in China on the Shanghai stock exchange, insider trading and manipulation appear as standard practices. Stocks rise and fall on rumors and not on company reports. Companies that promise to invest new capital in their operations sometimes use the money to speculate in real estate instead. The rules, where they exist, are openly flaunted. One observer commented that the difference between a lottery and the Shanghai stock market is that in the lottery one sometimes can get accurate information about the number before it is picked.

There are, of course, easier and safer approaches for an investor interested in emerging markets such as China. Since 1992, when shares for foreigners began to trade in China, more than a dozen Chinese companies have listed their shares in Hong Kong, another half dozen on the New York Stock Exchange, and a few more in Australia and Canada. Most of these are former state enterprises spun off by the government after adopting Western accounting standards. Even so, the early enthusiasm for China has been replaced with a good dose of caution.

Another option for people interested in emerging markets is to buy into a mutual fund. In 1995 there were at least seven China funds available to foreign investors. These funds tend to be small, and like any funds invested in volatile emerging markets, they can be trouble if investors flee and the managers then have to raise cash by dumping shares in companies that typically do not trade often.

There are also so-called closed-end China funds listed on Wall Street. Unlike regular mutual funds, which expand and contract as customers buy and sell, closed-end funds do not redeem shares. If investors want out, they have to sell their shares on an open market, which lowers their value but does not require their managers to dump stocks. Still another alternative is to find Western companies doing business in China. For instance, there are various Hong Kong conglomerates with stakes in mainland China.

The new and emerging global market for capital is hardly a safe haven for either investor or receiver of such investment. It can be a dangerous place, particularly when a loss of confidence strikes such a market. After all, it was not long ago that Mexico was one of the rising stars in the world's emerging markets. The country appeared to be doing everything right. In spite of this, Mexico's downfall came at the hands of international investors—the very people who ought to have been most impressed by the country's achievements.

Emerging country stock markets had already suffered steep declines in 1994, as we have noted. Rising American interest rates simply made investment in emerging markets less attractive. When Mexico's troubles became both acute and obvious emerging market falls continued and in some cases accelerated and there was a "flight to quality," as *The Economist* aptly describes.[2]

The ripple effects of the "flight to quality" hit the emerging markets with variable force. In Argentina during the first quarter of 1995, the stock market fell by 24 percent. To protect its markets from the meltdown, the country raised some $7 billion from, among others, the International Monetary Fund (IMF) and the World Bank in a bid to convince world markets that Argentina could avoid a devaluation.

A similar situation occurred in Brazil, whose currency also came under pressure. The central bank shifted and widened its exchange rate band, allowing the currency to drop. At the same time, Brazil sharply raised its short-term interest rate.

Like Mexico, Hungary devalued its currency, the forint, to encourage confidence in foreign investors. In Hungary the situation is particularly difficult due to a big budget deficit, which in turn prompted the government to announce deep cuts in social spending.

In Portugal, the government's hand was forced by the dangerous loss of market confidence, and the country's currency was abruptly devalued in March 1995. This is all the more striking since in Portugal the economic fundamentals seemed strong.

Of course, the increasing openness and globalization of capital markets is not the principal source of problems for these emerging countries. If foreign investors insist on moving their assets from, say, Mexican pesos to dollars, the central bank must play a critical role. Thus in 1994 Mexico's Central Bank provided the pesos that were needed to buy assets from foreign investors. The central bank purchased these assets directly and by extending credit to the banking system. That is, Mexico undertook a more expansionary monetary policy. In effect, the central bank converted into dollars the pesos obtained by foreigners. The resulting events produced a sharp drop in the country's foreign exchange reserves, hence a capital flight.

This process could go on until Mexico loses most of its reserves and thus forces a devaluation of the peso. When no further devaluation of the peso is expected by world investors, then confidence in the peso would be achieved. This is basically the way a regime of fixed exchange rates operates in principle. There is, in effect, a loss of reserves and/or a devaluation of the currency.

When a country denies economic reality for too long, something in the end must snap. By allowing the peso to depreciate earlier and so reducing the risk of future devaluation (as would be the case in a regime of properly floating exchange rates), the expected returns on peso assets would have been bolstered, and some modicum of investor confidence retained, and a currency crisis avoided.

In essence, the commitment to a fixed exchange rate regime is really a commitment to pursue a particular rule for monetary policy, a rule that involves fixing a particular price. For all practical purposes, a country has very limited room to pursue an independent monetary policy.

In practice, this means that there are only four ways a country can adjust to continuing changes in its balance of payments (in reality, changes in the demand and supply of its currency). One way, of course, is a change in the exchange rate. Another is a rise or fall in domestic prices. A third way is exchange controls and/or other controls over foreign transactions, including granting subsidies for exports and tariffs on imports. A fourth way is simply running up or down the amount of foreign exchange reserves available to the country.

If the objective is indeed free trade, then the third method (an imposition of controls) is ruled out. If the goal is fixed exchange rates, then the first method is also ruled out. In effect, the country is left with the second method, requiring declines or rises in internal prices and output. This method is not credible in today's world since it requires a country's central bank to stand aside and allow changes in the country's balance of payments to produce intolerable recession or inflation. The likely outcome would be trade controls and/or changes in the fixed exchange rate.

A fixed exchange rate system can represent a monetary regime for a single country, but not for the world. The world price level was determined in the 19th century by tying currencies to gold. In the post-World War II period, with the so-called Bretton Woods system, it was determined in effect by tying currencies to the dollar and American monetary policy.

For a single country, the argument for a fixed exchange rate system is really obvious. In fact, the pros and cons for such a system depend on, among other factors, the country's economic structure, objectives, and the nature and type of external forces to which it is subject. Moreover, governments and the public are imprecise as to what objectives the country is pursuing apart from usual (e.g., growth, stability, maximum employment). Structural factors such as country size, tradeable goods sector, capital mobility, and relative price 'flexibility may be important in reaching a decision on whether to adopt a particular exchange rate system. Similarly, the nature of disturbances to which a country is subject can influence the optimum exchange rate, such as shifts in foreign demand for the country's goods or securities or in the external terms of trade.

Another argument in favor of fixed exchange rates is that a commitment to a given rate avoids domestic monetary and fiscal disturbances that would otherwise take place. Accordingly, a discipline is imposed on economic policy that would be absent under a regime of freely floating exchange rates. In fact, some analysts consider this disciplinary effect in weak governments to be the strongest argument in favor of fixed exchange rates.[3]

It is, nevertheless, possible for a weak government to evade such discipline, if perhaps for a short period of time, by running down foreign exchange reserves. Under a system of freely floating exchange rates, these events would be quickly registered as a fall in the value of the country's currency. On the other hand, if the government and country are subject to strong internal and external pressures (as sometimes happens), a system of fixed exchange rates may be a useful defense against such pressures in part because fixed exchange rates may be easier to pursue technically. The technical tasks before the authorities are not made easier by the choice of which currency on which to fix the country's currency or basket of currencies in a multi-currency world.[4]

Much is made of the presumed ability of fixed exchange rates to reduce the perceived or subjective uncertainty of many economic agents. Variations in exchange rates impact negatively on some agents in that they feel thatan additional element of uncertainty is introduced in their transactions. The combination of political, economic, and psychological factors that influence capital move-ments—which in turn influence exchange rate movement—may prove over-whelming to some economic agents, whose experience may be limited to their own product and factor markets. Freely floating exchange rates may add another factor of uncertainty in their decision-making processes.

Hedging transactions against uncertainty is, of course, possible. It is nevertheless not always easy to do so, particularly if the time period is long and if forward exchange rates are themselves highly variable. Economic agents, moreover, are not likely to know whether observed movements in exchange rates are temporary or permanent, and they may not know the underlying structure of the economy in which they are operating. According to some analysts, the most important contribution of credibly fixed exchange rates may be to stabilize expectations and thereby inhibit erratic changes in behavior in response to scattered and incomplete information. To stabilize expectancy, however, a system of fixed exchange rates must have credibility. A pseudo-fixed exchange rate system in which changes are frequent will not meet the requirement for stabilizing expectations.[5] In any case, Milton Friedman pointed out in 1953 that destabilizing speculation is unlikely to last for the simple reason that it is not profitable.[6] Moreover, the uncertainty attributed to floating rates may be variability of the underlying fundamentals in a country's economy.

Some analysts argue that while it is correct that floating rates enable government exercise of discretionary monetary policy, such an exercise may not always be desirable. The more skeptical will add that experience suggests that such discretionary authority will more likely be abused than properly exercised. It is for this reason that they favor fixed rates. But should we have more faith in the foreign government of the country to which it pegs its own currency? Perhaps for small countries with limited, narrowly based economies a fixed exchange rate may reduce the volatility inherent in such economies. On the other hand, these same countries may experience serious problems due to the contemporary world's mixed system of "dirty floating" and pseudo-fixed exchange rates. This system can induce great financial instability for the small countries. For instance, if the currency of a major country—say, the dollar—appreciates relative to other major currencies (mark, pound, franc), then the dollar price of many of the small country's traded goods (exports, imports, and close substitutes) will decline, placing deflationary pressure not only on the traded goods but also, via substitution, on a broad range of goods and services. In any case, experience indicates that when perceived needs become pressing, the authorities will either suspend the commitment to fixed exchange rates or else inflate and thus break their commitment.

As for fiscal policy under a system of fixed exchange rates, the prospects for an independent policy, are better than for an independent monetary policy, provided, of course, that there is a market for a government's securities and that this market does not tie together both monetary policy and fiscal policy—which is typically the case in many less developed countries and emerging markets. The exercise of an independent fiscal policy is not a problem provided that the government can sell its securities at home and abroad. If countries cannot do so, then a commitment to fix exchange rates also reduces sharply the scope for an independent fiscal policy. In this event, the fiscal deficit is financed by the central bank, monetary and fiscal policies are joined, and autonomous fiscal and monetary expansion cannot be squared with fixed exchange rates

Clearly, these problems will likely be before policy makers and investors in emerging markets. In the long term, the prospects appear to be bright for emerging markets, though large disparities will remain between regions. Thus *The Economist*, for instance, reports that the increasingly globalized nature of trade and finance gives poor countries much to gain by pursuing sensible policies of reform.[7]

Most of the private investment going to emerging markets is confined to certain countries, with 87 percent in 1994 and early 1995 going to 20 nations led by China and then Mexico (a close second). Sub-Saharan Africa, on the other hand, got less than 1.5 percent. Even in sub-Saharan Africa, however, the complete picture is not all gloomy. Thus the region's GDP (gross domestic product) is forecast to rise by an average of 4.1 percent over the next decade, though rapid population growth means that GDP per person will grow by only 0.9 percent per year.

In relative terms, however, taking into account the population in each of the emerging market economies, the major recipients per capita in the period of 1990–1994 have been Singapore, with $16.400; Hong Kong, with $2,300; Hungary, with $1,200; Malaysia, with $1,000; and Argentina, with $800.[8] Singapore and Hong Kong are not really emerging markets but developed markets in their right. Their inflows reflect the strength of their financial markets, which intermediate and channel those flows to other countries (mainly South Asian countries and China). Thus it is that China has elected to list firms in Hong Kong rather than access international markets directly through issues of American depository receipts (ADRs) or global depository receipts (GDRs).

According to some observers, the reasons for the large increase in private flows abroad can be attributed to both external and internal factors.[9] External factors such as the reduction in short-term interest rates in some of the major world currencies lowered the external debt service to developing countries, thereby improving their solvency and credit rating and encouraging additional borrowing on their part.

At the same time, the economic downswing in the industrial countries and decline in short-term interest rates lowered the relative return on industrial countries' domestic capital. These developments encouraged the flow of funds into emerging markets, where returns were higher. Moreover, the increasing globalization and integration of international markets encouraged firms to move some activities into emerging markets where labor costs are lower. Finally, the industrialized countries have liberalized their own domestic markets which have made access to these markets possible to the developing countries, including their private firms. A good case in point is the liberalization of markets in the United States.

As for internal factors in the emerging market countries, analysts underscore that it is not only the size and the level of development in these countries but also the conduct of their political and economic policies, although in some instances political policies leave considerable room for improvement. The large differences in the flows of capital to different countries in good measure reflect differences in their internal economic as well as political policies.

According to Dehesa, the 16 emerging countries with the largest capital inflows have, with very few exceptions,

reached a reasonable degree of macroeconomic stability, have adopted successful price stabilization programs based on sound fiscal policies, have introduced institutional reforms liberalizing factor markets (notably, capital and labor), have reduced trade and investment barriers and, finally, have made important moves toward the privatization of state assets and the deregulation of financial markets.[10]

The net result of all these measures is to increase both the credibility of these emerging countries and the rate of return on their assets and investment projects. In a few of the countries, a full and credible stabilization and reform programs were not fully in place. In some of these countries, a tight monetary policy and increased domestic interest rates attracted large but speculative capital inflows. Such a development is made possible where a regime of fixed exchange rates permitted higher nominal returns on domestic financial assets, encouraging large but highly speculative and reversible capital imports. It is thus all the more important for a country to pursue credible policies if it is to encourage domestic investment and growth with the assistance of foreign capital. Proper policies will encourage the foreign capital inflows to finance a rise in investment spending, which, in the final analysis, is the only way to generate new resources to finance the service of the capital inflow in the future. A country's creditworthiness takes a short time to be lost and a long time to be reestablished. Improper domestic policies have a negative effect on the perception of creditworthiness held by foreign investors.

The World Bank, in search of a new role for itself, is now focusing on promoting private capital flows into emerging markets. It hopes to do so by encouraging these countries to develop a healthy, skilled work force and by encouraging good governance and a favorable regulatory environment for business. It hopes to use its expertise in a sort of "knowledge-based institution" to teach people how to form a society based on the rule of law, how to develop stock and bond markets and how to institute regulations that will help, not hinder, business.[11]

NOTES

1. George Macesich, *Integration and Stability: A Monetary View* (Westport, CT: Greenwood Press, 1995). For a review of the issues, also see Felix Rohatyn, "World Capital: The Need and the Risks," *New York Review of Books* (July 14, 1994), pp. 48–53.

2. *The Economist,* March 18, 1995, Vol. 334, Number 7906, p. 73.

3. See, for instance, Gottfried Haberler, "Integration and Growth of the World Economy in Historical Perspective," *American Economic Review*, 54, (March 1964), pp. 1–22.

4. See Matthew B. Canzoneri, "Exchange-Intervention Policy in a Multiple Country World," *Journal of International Economics*, 15 (November 1982), pp. 267–89.

5. For a useful discussion of issues under a system of fixed exchange rates, see Charles P. Kindleberger, "The Case for Fixed Exchange Rates," in *The International Adjustment Mechanism* (Boston: Federal Reserve Bank of Boston, 1970).

6. For a discussion of the case for flexible exchange rates, see Milton Friedman, "The Case for Flexible Exchange Rates," in Milton Friedman (ed.), *Essays in Positive Economics* (Chicago: University of Chicago Press, 1953), 157–203. See also Milton Friedman, "Free-Floating Anxiety," *National Review*, Vol. XLVI, No. 17 (12 September 1994), pp. 32–36.

7. *The Economist*, April 22, 1995, Vol. 335, No. 7911, p. 108.

8. Guillermo de la Dehesa, "The Recent Surge in Private Capital Flows to Developing Countries: Is It Sustainable?" Per Jacobsson Lecture, October 2, 1994, Madrid, Spain (Washington, DC: Per Jacobsson Foundation, International Monetary Fund, 1994), pp. 4–5.

9. Ibid.

10. Ibid., p. 9. The 16 major country recipients of private capital flows in 1990–1993 and total inflow in billions of U.S. dollars are Mexico, $52.8; China, $49.2; Argentina, $24.5; Korea, $22.9; Indonesia, $22.3; Malaysia, $19.2; Turkey, $19.0; Singapore, $18.2; Thailand, $18.1; Hungary, $14.7; Brazil, $14.4; Hong Kong, $13.6; Venezuela, $9.5; Chile, $5.4; India, $5.4; Philippines, $5.3. Ibid., p. 5.

11. Paul Lewis, "A New World Bank: Consultant to Third World Investors," *The New York Times*, April 27, 1995, p. CA.

3

East and Central Europe:
Marx and Markets

INVESTOR PREFERENCE FOR ASIA AND LATIN AMERICA

To judge from available evidence, the world registered approximately $380 billion in private capital flows during the period 1990–1993. The share of East and Central European countries amounted to approximately $15 billion for the same period. Clearly, this amount is far less than was expected five years earlier.

The reasons appear to be in the competition for capital. Opportunities for investment and returns in Asian countries, for instance, are more attractive than in the East and Central European countries. The same is also true for Latin American countries. In addition, both Asia and Latin America have functioning market economies, while the countries in East and Central Europe are on a rather uncertain transition path to restructuring their economies (and political systems) to meet the requirements of a market economy.

Another reason may be the geographical preferences of private investors. American investors have a preference for Latin America and some countries in Southeast Asia and China. Japanese investors prefer Asia. It is the American investors who have a stronger preference, compared to other foreign investors, for the countries of East and Central Europe. The smaller German flow of funds to this region can be accounted for in part by the heavy German involvement in the former East Germany and in part by the unsettled conditions in the countries of the region. As the processes of transition continue and conditions improve in these countries, they may receive larger inflows of capital.

IMPROVING THE INVESTMENT CLIMATE

The societies in East and Central Europe are in transition, though it is not clear that this transition is to democracy. This underscores what should be clear by now: although societies do change, it is a myth to think that they can be turned upside down—at least not peacefully. The continuities between before and after the removal of Marxist communism in the region are striking.

The several countries in the region (and in the Soviet Union, including Russia, even earlier) had mostly authoritarian rule before 1945. The removal of communism alone will not bring democracy. Societies change only slowly. Whatever measures are undertaken to improve the investment climate must take into account the nature of these societies. Potential investors should and will do so as well.

Consider, for instance, the important phase of democracy dealing with forming political parties and writing and adopting constitutions. On paper, each country has numerous parties. A closer reading will indicate that most are no more than names.[1] *The Economist* arranges the more familiar parties from left to right on the conventional spectrum.[2] A few ex-communists (now called socialists) and a few social democrats are now in the parliaments. The center-left and center-right are for capitalism. The center-left favors welfare and civil liberties. The center-right, which includes Christian parties, is more traditional.

Even so, the designation of left and right is not always clear. Some so-called left-wing parties push for strong free market arrangements; some right-wing ones want more state intervention. The term, *conservative* more often than not means old-time Marxist communist. Still other parties defy any left-right line (e.g., Bulgaria's Turkish party, Hungary's freeholders, Romania's Hungarian party, and Slovakia's Slovenia and Croatia nationalists).

As for the constitutional issues and, in particular, how power is divided between president and parliament and how the rights of minorities are protected, theory does not assure practice. In particular, the issue of protecting minorities in these countries leaves much to be desired. Measures for the protection of individual rights and promotion of the rights of ethnic groups are unclear.

These issues faced these same countries more than 70 years ago. None, with one or two exceptions, handled these issues in a satisfactory manner. Perhaps these countries have learned something. They may not all be at the beginning. At the very least, the starting point has changed, as has the general West European environment, which now appears more democratic than earlier. Nevertheless, the tasks of building democracy and a free market economy with a favorable and secure investment climate in the region are formidable.

In fact, in no small measure the poor investment climate in these post-communist societies can be attributed to the outbursts of nationalist politics and ethnic strife. With the collapse of the containing structure which the political arrangements of that period provided, people are now freer to act out ancient grievances. Ethnic hatreds can be kept simmering from generation to generation, providing a reservoir of hostile biases and bitter memories of historic grievances that are shared by members of an ethnic group and can set off active antagonism in times of group hardships or under the prodding of an irresponsible and self-serving leadership.

Scholars in general agree that unlike race, ethnicity is less a matter of common genes than of shared history, perception, group identity and grievances. Some of the strongest and most violent divides run between people of the same stock (e.g., people in northern Ireland and the former Yugoslavia). In both instances, there are telling historic differences in the several combatants.

I have discussed elsewhere the role of nationalism and the importance of investment in materialism by people.[3] In many respects, the dislike of people from other ethnic groups is a byproduct of investment in one's own nationality and ethnic identity. In fact, when differences between groups are small (e.g., Serbs and Croats or between northern and southern Irish), greater emphasis is placed on minor distinguishing features, such as religions. This is a phenomenon well known to ethnic scholars and psychiatrists as the narcissism of minor differences. In effect, the closer the resemblance between neighboring groups, the greater the resources (including emotion) people must invest in maintaining small differences.

As economists suggest, collective goods are important to a people and their socioeconomic and political organization. One such good is collective memory of a people's past glories and traumas. Collective memory is one way for a people to keep its identity alive, as well as to pass it on to future generations. It is also possible for a society to overinvest as well as underinvest in the good of collective memory, with tragic consequences. Failure to invest and share in such memory risks branding an individual as a traitor to the group. Overinvestment in collective memory may serve as a continual source of friction, eroding the foundation of society. Inflammatory leaders will always be on board to push ethnic antagonisms and an ideology that promises a brighter future if the group's enemies are destroyed.

COPING WITH ETHNIC POLITICS

The disintegrating quality of ethnic strife is understood by the intransigence of its politics. This ethnification of politics involves several interrelated strategies.[4] Their underlying tie is the dominant cleavage that ethnicity plays. There is, first, the strategy of drawing territorial boundaries to maximize ethnic homogeneity; second, the pursuit of policies that underscore the status rights of citizens according to ethnic groups; and third, the organization of politics, policies, and organizations aimed at promoting one ethnic group while excluding those outside the group.

The ethnification of politics is particularly rampant in the former socialist countries of Europe, although other areas of the world are by no means excluded. The political leadership in many of these countries views ethnification as perfectly rational. Attempts to persuade these people that a course of action is contrary to Western and accepted standards of political behavior and that it is not consistent with the standards of civilized behavior to which they presumably aspire meet with little success.

If the political personalities are aware of the disastrous consequences of their ethnification of politics, why pursue such a course of action? There are apparently rational reasons for doing so. First, in the former socialist countries the current leadership is typically tainted by association with the former regimes, which typically suppressed ethnic extremes. The current leadership now uses ethnicity as a means of distancing itself from the former regime. The stronger the ties to the former regime, the more nationalist the new political leadership.

It is not surprising that the economic crises characteristic of these countries enforce the leadership's desire to adopt a policy of protectionism rather than of free trade. To these ends, secure frontiers are necessary to protect the outflow of existing resources and inflow of migrants, refugees, and other problems.

Secure frontiers require a strong state to enforce them. With the wobbly nature of many of these states and their governments' inability to enforce the frontiers, the leadership typically turns to ethnic inclusion and exclusion. As a result, people identify each other by ethnicity rather than citizenship. One consequence of the breakdown of state authority and police power is that those minority citizens without a strong and nearby patron state are at risk.

Regimes in these former socialist states were ideologically future oriented; the current leadership attempts to distance itself by adopting and cultivating a distant and mystic past. This is to serve in place of an absent and credible program of reconstruction and political and social integration. The practices of recasting old symbols, including flags, currency, and other trappings from a golden era ar standard. Unfortunately, for a number of these socialist successor states this involves celebrating a fascist and/or equally odious past (e.g., Croatia and Slovakia).

The previous regimes in these countries managed to destroy whatever institutions of autonomous collective action existed before the communists came to power. Various church organizations managed to survive if not prosper under the communists. As a result, churches tend to provide some modicum of guidance and focus in an otherwise associational wasteland. It is little wonder that ethnicity and materialism now serve as guidance for collective action. In effect, they have displaced the state-dependent organizations and the authoritarian mobilization of collective action.

The ethnification of politics and intolerance toward other groups may be driven by the rational calculational that no fair and stable solutions of ethnic conflict are possible, whether agreed upon by groups in question or imposed from the outside. This indeterminacy is reinforced by the urgency with which the various ethnic groups now view the distribution of territory, sovereignty, and other resources. They may consider it appropriate to lay claim to what they consider as rightfully theirs.

As to why there is no fair and impartial way to settle ethnic conflict, observers note that given the mixed populations in many areas in question, as in Europe, it is impossible to draw territorial boundaries around homogeneous populations. Moreover, a democratic process for reaching an equitable solution to ethnic conflict is not at hand. It is available only after the relevant universe of those entitled to vote has been established—but which ethnic group will be given the right to vote? The human rights approach, whether focused on individual and/or collective rights will yield unsatisfactory results because it is difficult if not impossible to draw a line at which all the rights of a minority are met and none of the rights of the majority are violated.

In sum, resolving ethnic conflict by resort to boundaries, votes, and human rights, whether individual or collective, is not likely to produce a stable solution

given the issues involved. Little wonder that force is used in settling the argument, as in the Yugoslav civil war and elsewhere. It is also not surprising that the logic of national political nihilism is now dominant in many areas of the world caught up in ethnic strife and that in such regions and countries the atmosphere discourage investment.

MARX AND MARKETS

It will take considerable time for these countries to rid themselves of the economic, political, and psychological drag of their past immersion in Marxism. The attractiveness of Marxist-socialist-communist ideology was based on the belief that it could and would create a society free from want. In many respects, it was the byproduct of the Industrial Revolution and capitalism as it was practiced at that time. In fact, Karl Marx focused on the inequities that the Industrial Revolution cast up. Communism proclaimed the building of God's kingdom on earth and happiness of humankind. It simply could not deliver on its promises. Instead it promoted a tightly controlled economic and political system run by the Communist Party. No withering away of the state and no emancipation of the proletariat occurred.

It is in Karl Marx's *Das Kapital* that one finds the basis for much of communist dogma. Useful insights may be gained by considering the essential elements of his theory.[5] Unlike the utopian reformers (e.g., Robert Owen, 1771–1858), Karl Marx (1818–1883) coupled scholarship with revolutionary agitation. It is not enough, according to Marx, to theorize; one must build a revolutionary party capable of seizing power when capitalism collapses. He did not suffer lightly other socialists who happened to disagree with his views. In fact, he established the practice of the vitriolic denunciation of opposing views that burdens so much of recent past and contemporary socialist literature.

In Marx's view, capitalism (a term he invented) is doomed. His demonstration of its demise draws on so-called laws of motion of capitalist society. On one level Marx bases his argument on the inherent injustices of capitalism that lead ultimately to economic and social conditions that cannot be maintained. At another level his argument is sociological in that class conflict between increasingly affluent capitalists and an increasingly miserable working class will break out in social revolution. At still another level the argument is economic in that accumulation of capital in private hands, while creating increasing abundance, also leads to the inevitable breakdown of capitalism. At all three levels the idea of conflict is underscored: conflict between ideal and reality—the moral issue; conflict between labor and capital—the sociological issue; and conflict between growth and stagnation—the economic issue. This conflict generates change, and so capitalism, according to Marx, must eventually give way to another social system in which conflict is replaced by ethical, social, and economic harmony. This change is the "dialectical process" whereby socialism will replace capitalism. Thus Marx created one of the world's most powerful ideologies, whose vision of

abundance, equality, and freedom stood in challenge to classical-liberal individualism, private property, and private enterprise.

The rise of socialism, the demand for social justice, and Marx's use of such instruments of the dominant ideology as the labor theory of value and the theory of capital accumulation to attack its legitimacy—all prompted a search for a theoretical defense of the existing system. In part, the new defense presented is that of the philosophy of the individual developed and cultivated largely by dominant business and economic interests from the mid-19th century up to and beyond World War II. In effect, it is a reinforced version of the familiar laissez-faire argument long known to scholars.

Economists for the most part did not take the extreme position of individualism and laissez faire very seriously. For one thing, Benthamite utilitarianism (Jeremy Bentham, 1748–1832) suggested that government intervention may on occasion be justified by the greatest-good argument. For another, economists concerned themselves with pressing social issues for which the philosophy of extreme individualism provided little insight. This did not mean, however, that economists rejected the individual philosophy. On the contrary, they remained within its general framework.

More important, economists intentionally or otherwise developed a new theoretical apparatus that presumably serves to refute the Marxian critique of capitalism. This is the neoclassical economies developed since 1870. In effect, the foundation of economics is reduced to the desires and wants of the individual, and the whole theoretical explanation of production, distribution, and prices is based on the single assumption of rational individual self-interest. Neoclassical economics is a significant scientific advance since it reduces to the simple but elegant idea of marginalism a complex set of separate theories of value, distribution, and returns to factors of production. The value of a product or service is not the result of the amount of labor embodied in it, but of the usefulness of the last unit purchased. With marginalism a new approach to economics developed.

Carl Menger (1840–1921), William Stanley Jevons (1835–1882), Leon Walras (1837–1910), and Alfred Marshall (1842–1924) shifted the focus of economics from social classes and their economic interests underscored by David Ricardo (1772–1823) and Karl Marx to that of the individual. The individual consumer became a centerpiece of the theoretical apparatus of economics, displacing the principle of economic distribution envisioned by Ricardo as the mainspring of economic progress and on which Marx based his theory of the breakdown of capitalism. The system of free markets does maximize individual welfare. Since consumers are assumed to maximize their satisfaction and since production responds to consumer wants, it follows that the result will be welfare maximizing. Moreover, marginalism also shows that the costs of production are pushed to the lowest level possible by competition. If allowed to operate without constraints, the entire economy becomes a pleasure-maximizing machine in which the differences between consumer benefits and production costs are increased to the highest level possible. In short, economics becomes transformed into a service consistent with the individualist social philosophy of Herbert Spencer and William Summers Graham.

The development also served to reinforce, at least in the United States, the legal theories of U.S. Supreme Court Justice Stephen Field (1816–1899) and the philosophy of unrestricted individualism in U.S. constitutional law. One result of Field's interpretation was to eliminate much state legislation dealing with economic affairs, including the regulation of hours of work, child labor, and factory conditions. Private property is thus viewed as a natural right that no government can interfere with lightly.

Marx's challenge is also taken up in the application of marginal analysis to income distribution, which demonstrates that factors of production—labor, land, and capital—earn a wage exactly equal to their contribution to the value of output. Called the theory of marginal productivity and based on the last marginal unit, its conclusion is that workers would be paid a wage qual to the last unit of output they produced. The same idea is applied to profits earned from capital and to rent from land. In effect, to each factor of production the same law applied. No one could exploit anyone else since everyone received what he or she deserved. The entire product is exhausted and no surplus value exists. Marx's concerns are simply irrelevant.

This happy state of affairs, critics are quick to point out, depends on the assumptions of marginal productivity theory. In the first instance, the theory rests on the assumption of perfect competition. Second, all factors of production must be completely substitutable for one another. Third, there must be no change in costs of production per unit of output as the level of production falls or rises. Not all economists are satisfied by such assumptions. Indeed, some economists have never accepted the theory of marginal productivity, which they view as singularly unreal.

It is the issue of periodic booms and depressions which seems to plague the rapidly industrializing countries and which attracted considerable public and government attention. During the first half of the 19th century, most economists showed little concern for this issue due to their acceptance of the general proposisions of Say's Law of Markets (J. B. Say, 1767–1832), according to which there should be no periodic economic breakdowns and the economy should continue to operate at uninterrupted high levels of output and employment. Say's Law states that demand is created by production, and in the aggregate the two can never get out of phase with one another. Economists interested in business cycles typically sought causes outside the framework of production and distribution.

Stanley Jevons (1835–1882), for instance, developed a quantitative relationship between sunspots and business fluctuations, arguing that these fluctuations are connected with periodic variations of weather affecting all parts of the earth, and probably arising from increased waves of heat received from the sun at average intervals of ten years. This serves simply to reinforce Say's Law, since the "cause" is outside the system of production and distribution. Perhaps the best interpretation within Say's Law is provided by the argument that the monetary system generates instability while the basic system of production and distribution is stable. Stabilize the monetary and financial system, and general economic stability is assured.

In 1873 Walter Bagelot, in his now classic on money and finance, *Lombard Street*, spelled out how in his view stabilization was to be done: Limit the expansion of credit to legitimate needs of business through effective action by the central bank. This will prevent excessive credit issue from overstimulating the economy and thus developing into a crisis. Once the situation gets out of hand, the central bank can probably moderate the crisis, but the economy will simply have to weather out the storm.

These theoretical advances served, among other things, to entrench capitalism firmly and defend it from its critics. Marginal utility, marginal productivity, and the monetary theory of business cycles supplemented the basic analysis of classical economics. The free enterprise economy is pictured as operating to produce what consumers want, thus maximizing welfare, distributing products justly, and normally operating at full utilization of resources. The issue of laissez faire in neoclassical economics is not a rigidly held doctrine. In fact, the major area of exception is monetary policy, which is assigned to the government and its agent, the central bank. It is their responsibility to preserve economic stability by properly managing the money supply to serve the legitimate needs of business.

This is interpreted to mean the needs of production and distribution. The banking school influence here, in the form of the "real bills" doctrine (lending on tangible goals), is obvious. Even so, such monetary intervention is to be held to a minimum and strictly guided by the free market. In short, discretionary monetary policy is to be limited by the requirements of the free market and the constraints imposed on it by the gold standard. As a result, the scope for the exercise of discretionary authority by central banks is limited.

Neoclassical economists also approve other types of government intervention which facilitate the operation of free competition and free markets. On this score, concern with monopolies and legislation designed to control their practices tend to be supported by most economists. The fact is that neoclassical economics does tend to adopt "lock, stock, and barrel" simple individualism and laissez faire, as critics assert; it does not opt for wholesale intervention. It accommodates the realistic needs of society and has strong ideological implications, since it serves to rebuild the theory of free private enterprise on a new basis, thereby making the refutation of Marx unnecessary. Private prosperity and free private enterprise weathered the Marxist storm more or less intact, thanks to the efforts of neoclassical economists.

The liberal reform philosophies of several past U.S. presidential administrations managed to restructure much of America's economic and social framework without gross violations of individualism, private property rights, and the market-oriented private enterprise economy. Events took a less satisfactory course in the former Soviet Union and in the countries of East and Central Europe during and following the two world wars. War, revolution, and counterrevolution served to wreck what appeared to be promising liberal reforms that began at the turn of the century and continued, albeit in a halting fashion, into World War I.

At the time, Russia was one among the more backward countries in Europe. It had a primitive agriculture and industry staffed, for the most part, by an illiterate population. By professing its allegiance to a Marxist ideology, which postulated that socialism would naturally evolve in highly industrialized economies in which the working class comprised the majority of the population, Russia was simply at odds with received socialist doctrine. The country simply did not square with what Karl Marx and his followers had in mind. To complicate matters, the world revolution had failed and the new Soviet state was surrounded by antagonistic capitalist countries who considered it an "illegitimate child of history," as Winston Churchill put it.

V. I. Lenin (1870–1924) led the Bolshevik Revolution to a successful conclusion. He did so after convincing his followers that Russia could bypass the capitalist industrial era and move directly from an agricultural semifeudal society into the socialist era. It was Lenin who formulated the basic idea of how to accomplish the goal of a socialist era. In essence, rapid and large-scale industrialization of Russia would serve as a means for building the working-class society in which socialism could flourish. This required an alliance between workers and peasants under a worker's dictatorship, although priority was given to the construction of an urban and industrial society. Lenin died before his strategy was translated into specific programs of action. A debate on goals and means continued in the 1920s and into the 1930s, when Stalin ended discussion with the first purge trials, which were to shake the foundations of the new Soviet state.

Joseph Stalin (1879–1953) manipulated the great urbanization-industrialization debate to his favor. The moderates, led by the leading Marxist theoretician Nikolai Bukharin, argued for balanced economic development and the postponement of world revolution until the Soviet state was strong enough domestically to support such a revolution successfully. Although urbanization and industrialization were to be encouraged, it was dangerous for the Soviet state to push the peasants too far and to threaten further their loyalty to the regime. In short, a slower development pace tuned to the realistic possibilities of the Soviet state was prudent. Stalin called this approach the *right deviation*.

Opposing the moderates was the so-called left wing of the Communist Party led by Leon Trotsky (1879–1940), who, in fact, was Lenin's key man during the Bolshevik Revolution. The idea pushed by the left wing called for mobilizing the country's economy to the utmost, squeezing living standards in order to free resources for industrial development, and using the power of the state to extract the maximum surplus from agriculture, which was to be collectivized and mechanized. In effect, the economy was to be deliberately unbalanced to force industrialization. As for the international scene, the Soviet state would never be secure in a capitalist world. As a result, it could best protect itself by exporting world revolution, principally by demonstrating the superior productivity of socialism through economic growth.

Stalin, at first, took the position of supporting rapid industrialization and forced-draft development advocated by the left wing, but he ruled against collectivization of agriculture to avoid alienating the peasants. As for world revolution, he sided with the moderates and Bukharin, forming an alliance that drove Trotsky into exile. Stalin then sided with the left and opted for a collectivization of agriculture and a rapid rate for the accumulation of capital beyond anything called for by Trotsky and his faction. This was enough to gain for Stalin the support necessary to purge Bukharin. In essence, the debate resolved into the establishment of ambitious development goals and a planning apparatus to carry them out, with the Stalin dictatorship the driving force of the system.

This is the Soviet model with more or less appropriate modification imposed on East and Central European countries following World War II. It was also the model and system dropped by Josef Broz Tito (1892–1980) and Yugoslavia following the Tito-Stalin split in 1948. With the departure of Yugoslavia on its own independent road to socialism in its unique model of worker self-management, a new chapter in socialism began. The socialist world would not be the same again.

By 1995 the Soviet Union, Yugoslavia, and Czechoslovakia were no more. Their successor states and others in East and Central Europe have gone their own way. Their conversion to a free private market economy and democracy will likely take years even with outside assistance, and there is no guarantee that it will ever happen. The problem of ethnic strife is replicated in one form or another, as we have discussed, in all of the successor states, and their fragmentation on ethnic and/or religious lines is possible. Many of these successor states already have authoritarian regimes, and others may well be on their way to one. In any event, they are not likely to attract the type of external investment that would facilitate their transition to modern, viable economies.

WHAT CAN BE DONE

There is little disagreement that, overall, the former socialist countries of East and Central Europe face tremendous difficulties in improving the region's investment climate. The 1989 fall of the socialist system has ushered in a host of problems, including the rule of law, of public liberties, of private property rights, and of a private market economy. Everywhere the totalitarian experience of decades has made a rational solution to these outstanding problems extremely difficult.

Some argue that history has come to an end and a new world order consisting of liberal democratic ideals and free market economies has arrived. More likely, history is far from being over and the former socialist countries (like it or not) will have to strain to accommodate to world economic and financial markets, which have become increasingly integrated. Many of these countries were worse off after the fall of socialism than before, although there does not appear any ground swell for a return to the type of socialism practiced earlier.

The old communist regimes cannot be brought back. Thanks to the ethnification and fragmentation of politics and politicians apparently incapable of making choices and decisions, the reform and transformation processes in these countries are fragile. The draft toward authoritarianism is real enough.

The problems and issues are clear. The transition from a repressive but predictable system to a private market economy demands private initiative. Privatization has proven to be much more difficult than thought. In countries that once guaranteed full employment, there is now high unemployment. High unemployment and increased income disparities have caused social discontent. In most of these countries, the bureaucracies have resisted change and former party members have used their advantages as newly minted "democrats" to enrich themselves and their friends.

Financial and monetary organization has proven to be a particularly serious problem in the transition processes. In a market economy, bank credit is allocated on the basis of the creditworthiness of firms. In the former socialist economies, credit from banks tended to flow to those firms with the best political connections. Now, those that get the credit are large firms whose managers come from the same ex-communist network as the bank directors.

In spite of the difficulties some progress has been made toward a market economy.[6] In some of the former socialist countries, industrial production at least stopped falling in 1995. Most have stuck with their reform and stabilization programs. Inflation has been reduced in many of these countries, as has unemployment. Economic growth is coming from small private businesses, especially small retail firms. Some were started through local auctions and sale of small state enterprises, while others were started by new owners. As we noted private foreign investment, particularly in joint ventures, has increased in several of the countries.

NOTES

1. For a good discussion of the issues, see "Democracy in Eastern Europe," *The Economist*, February 1, 1992, pp. 52–53.

2. Ibid., p. 53.

3. George Macesich, *Economic Materialism and Stability* (New York: Praeger, 1985), pp. 1-20.

4. See, for instance, Claus Offe, "Strong Causes, Weak Cures," *East European Constitutional Reviews* Vol. I, No. 1 Spring 1992, pp. 21–23.

5. Karl Marx, *Das Kapital* (New York: Modern Library, Inc., 1906).

6. See, for instance, Ž. Puhovski, I. Prpić, and D. Vojnić (eds.), *Politics and Economics of Transition* (Zagreb: Informator, 1993).

4

Latin America:
Stumbling into the 1990s

THE DIFFICULT YEARS

Latin America's difficult years in the first half of the 1990s managed to erode much of the economic gains achieved in the 1960s. Inflation has plagued the region. In some of the countries (Argentina, Brazil, Peru, Bolivia), inflation exceeded more than 1,000 percent a year. Economic collapse in a number of the countries (e.g., Argentina) prompted introduction of new currencies. Heavy foreign borrowing in the 1970s in the region, encouraged by high prices for such domestic products as oil and coffee and the subsequent pledging of revenue from these commodities for debt repayment, produced a false sense of security. When the world prices for these and other commodities sharply declined in the 1980s, the Latin American countries were left with a debt they could not repay. Economic growth declined and for most Latin America was negative. Unemployment and social unrest rose.

In effect, inflation, foreign trade problems (including a large foreign debt), population growth beyond what the countries can meaningfully absorb into the labor force, increased inequality, and corruption (which often permeates all strata of Latin American society and is firmly lodged in the region's cultural heritage) are serious obstacles for the free flow of investment into the area. There is little assurance that prospects for Latin America will improve in the short term. Many of these problems are common to other regions (e.g., East and Central Europe, Africa). Unlike other regions, however, the United States has close interests in Latin America.

MEXICO: AN EXAMPLE

Mexico is of increasing importance to the United States for a number of reasons. Mexico is one of the three major trading partners of the United States. It is also one with which the United States has a trade surplus. The new North American Free Trade Agreement (NAFTA) includes the United States, Canada, and Mexico, and promises to compete seriously with the European Community.

Mexico's oil supply assures alternative sources of oil, which can reduce dependence on the uncertain Middle Eastern supply. Of course, Mexico has taken important steps in opening its economy to private foreign investment.

The country's problems characterize Latin America-and other regions as well. Population growth has eased, but it is still growing faster than the economy's ability to absorb the increase. A safety valve, of course, has been the flow of Mexican migrants to the United States. complicating relations between the two countries. Mexico's foreign debt is less a problem than in the 1980s; but it still places pressure on Mexico to export more and thus increase foreign exchange, which is needed to service the debt. The income distribution in Mexico assures potential social unrest. Corruption continues to be a problem for Mexico as well for the current and potential foreign investors.

Mexico can be placed among other emerging markets such as Brazil, Hungary, and Venezuela. It is probably slightly ahead (in terms of per capita income) of some of the emerging markets in countries of Central and East Europe. It is also subject to more external economic influences, due in good part to its oil industry. In the 1970s, this industry served to generate the foreign exchange necessary to finance domestic Mexican development. As long as prospects for oil were bright, so was Mexico's future. When oil prices dropped in the 1980s, Mexico's external debt soared.

In fact, Mexico's development strategy owes much to its oil industry. Oil served this strategy in much the same fashion as copper in other Latin American countries to raise living standards. The strategy could be used for industrialization purposes as well as to raise living standards. For instance, Middle Eastern oil-producing countries use much of their oil revenues to raise living standards and less for strict industrial development.

Mexico, Brazil, Argentina, and other Latin American countries have also resorted to import substitution as a development strategy. This involves the promotion of domestic production of goods and services that displace imports. There is, of course, a downside to such a strategy, for which Latin America has paid. Prices for domestic products are often higher than for imported items as a consequence of reduced competition.

In terms of development strategies, it is useful to note the way East Asian countries viewed the problem of development in the post-World War II period. These countries focused on the export of manufactured goods, a slow process of growth development since it involves improvement of labor and managerial skills. The export surplus generated was used for further domestic and export development. Of course, the strategy involves sacrifices for domestic consumers since resources are used for the most part in pushing this development of export-oriented industries. Such a process has led observers to note that East Asian consumers have not always been served by their governments.

Mexico adopted the import substitution strategy early in the post-World War II period, when this strategy was particularly popular. The net result was that the Mexican consumer was forced to pay, through higher prices for goods and services, for the forced industrialization of the country. Government intervention with the economy was significant. Exchange controls, import quotas, and restrictions placed serious burdens on the economy.

Due to world price increases for oil in the 1970s, the Mexican oil industry received a stimulus and the country soon became an important player on the world oil market. Ostensibly the increased oil revenues were to be used to improve the country's infrastructure as well as to provide an improved standard of living for the poor. In fact, the earnings were for the most part expended on grandiose projects and outright graft, underscoring the centuries-old problem of corruption in Mexico.

The extent of the Mexican government's intervention in the economy since the 1930s is well documented.[1] The Mexican government was probably well ahead of many other Latin American countries. For instance, by 1938, the government owned or controlled the oil industry Petroleum de Mexico, S.A. (PEMEX), most of the electric power industry, steel production, and financial organizations; and it subsidized and controlled social overhead facilities, including ports, roads, and other facilities. Foreign ownership of industry was strictly prescribed and controlled. In effect, economic nationalism was the order of the day.

What are we to make of these efforts on the part of Mexico and its government? From about 1949 to 1978, the economy expanded tenfold in terms of GNP, and Mexico rose from a very poor and less developed country to a developing country. Then in the 1980s, disaster struck with a decline in world oil prices of about 70 percent. In short order, Mexico's foreign debt created serious problems; the country's currency was devalued, inflation increased, the economy deteriorated, and political radicalism grew.

By the end of the 1980s, measures to turn around Mexico's economy resulted in efforts to privatize the economy. By 1992, Mexico had merged, liquidated, or sold more than 800 of the better than 1100 state enterprises and completed the sale of mine-owned banks as well as steel mills and mines. In fact, all state enterprises were on the auction block except the state-owned oil company PEMEX.

Foreign investment in Mexico was reconsidered. Measures were taken to remove early restrictions on foreign investment, some of which had been in place since the Mexican Revolution of 1910. Many of these restrictions were ostensibly designed to prevent U.S. dominance of the Mexican economy. One consequence was that Mexico had the lowest rate of foreign investment of any Latin American country. Since 1988 and the easing and removal of restrictions on foreign investment in the country, Mexico has registered significant increases in direct foreign investment (for the most part by U.S. firms).

Even so, poverty remains one of the country's dominant characteristics. Depending on one's choice of estimates, more than 20 percent of Mexican households in 1984 received incomes of little more than $3 a day, considered at the time sufficient to cover the basic essentials for an average household. By 1989, real living standards slipped even further. When a division is made between moderate poverty and extreme poverty, one estimate reports more than 20 percent of the population, or 17 million people, living in extreme poverty in 1987.

Mexico's income distribution provides additional insight into its problems. The distribution favors wealthy Mexicans whose wealth is concentrated in real estate or invested abroad. It was not too long ago that a few families in Mexico owned or controlled much of the land, due in good part to the carryover from the latifundium system of the last century. Even though the Revolution of 1910 broke up the latifundium system, many of the families retained their wealth.

Industrialization of the 1960s and 1970s provided increased jobs and wages for people in the lower end of the income distribution scale. Nevertheless, the chief beneficiaries appear to be the wealthy and upper-middle classes. Import substitution kept out imports and stimulated Mexican business and so created jobs. Nonetheless, a few of the large, capital-intensive Mexican firms appear to be the principal beneficiaries.

Tax evasion and avoidance are another problem in Mexico. The tax system itself is probably more regressive than progressive. One consequence is that the social welfare benefits are also minimal. To this may be added the country's ongoing battle with corruption. This is not surprising, given the nature of single-political-party countries. On this score, Mexico is a good example. The country has had a single-party political system since 1929, when the Partido Revolucianario Institucional (PRI) was established. The opportunities for corruption and outright theft that arose should not be underestimated. Many of the recent political reforms are viewed by observers as more symbolic than substantive, designed to improve Mexico's political image in the United States and Latin America, especially when trade and financial agreements are concerned.

LATIN AMERICA'S OTHER EXAMPLES

The Mexican government has attempted to battle corruption and related issues through the creation of a human rights commission, the Commesion Nacional de Derechos Humanos (CNDH), which has cracked down in the 1990s on a number of government employees for taking bribes. On these issues and particularly human rights, other Latin American countries are not too different from Mexico. Peru and Chile are but two cases in point. The military forces in these two countries are as reluctant as any to give up their influence.

Peru's government approved a broad amnesty law that absolves members of the military of all human rights abuses committed during its 15-year war with Leftist guerrillas. This law was denounced by human rights groups, the victims' relatives, and the U.S. government, which said that the amnesty showed that Peru was not seriously committed to protecting human rights.

In Chile, the military defied judicial authority by preventing the government from arresting two former secret police officials after the Supreme Court upheld prison sentences for them in May 1995 for their ordering the murder of Orlando Letellier, a prominent Chilean opposition leader, in Washington in 1976.[2] President Eduardo Frei of Chile called on the nation's institutions to comply with the high court's ruling. But General Augusto Pinochet, the former dictator who is still commander in chief of the army, said that the trial of the officers had been unjust and that they had to be protected from public humiliation. Many observers considered the military's defiance of civilian authority as a technical coup.

In the view of some observers in human right groups, democracy in Latin America will not mature unless it is respected by all institutions in society. As long as normal citizens perceive that state agents are above the law and that some people are immune from prosecution or are not held accountable, democracy and its related institutions, including private property, are on uncertain grounds.

Latin American countries share a number of characteristics which are very difficult to overcome. In mid-1995, Mexico, then in the process of overhaul of its notoriously corrupt judicial system (as part of a promise to strengthen the rule of law), was presumably stunned by news that a Mexico City judge, Abraham Polo Uscanga, was murdered. This was the third such murder within weeks of prominent people who had questioned the promises of judicial reform in the country.[3] In Colombia, the authorities were apparently successful in reducing by at least one the number of drug traffickers in the country.[4]

These difficulties are underscored in the important area of privatization. From Mexico to Brazil to Argentina, countries in the region are seeking foreign investors to run former government monopolies like power generation and telecommunications. As American companies take up the task, they are too often confronted by the old nationalist passions that led to widespread seizures of foreign-owned utilities in the 1960s and 1970s.[5] These indicents are a warning to foreign investors about the hazards of operating in a region that is starting to open politically sensitive public utilities to foreign investment.

Venezuela is an example of the complicated and politically sensitive issue of privatization in Latin America. In Venezuela, the consortium Venworld, led by GTE, paid $1.9 billion for a 35-year controlling concession of the country's telephone company in 1991. The president at the time, Carlos Andrés Pérez, was a free market advocate who welcomed the foreign involvement. Two coups attempts, four changes of government, and seven communications ministers later, the country's new president, Rafael Caldera, often follows policies at odds with those of Mr. Pérez, his lifelong political rival. And in Congress the debate has continued whether CANTV should have been privatized to begin with.

The hostility of some Latin American politicians is only one among other problems that foreign investors face. There are also the xenophobic Latin American labor unions. In Venezuela, the union leaders were opposed from the outset to privatization to the extent of trying to disrupt the ceremony granting foreign investors the telephone concession in 1991. Led by the Radical Cause Party, the unions have also tried to block GTE's merit-based management system, preferring the political criteria that prevailed in the old state-company days.

Beyond the political issues, CANTV's management has had to cope with Venezuela's serious economic problems, including the collapse of half of the country's banking sector in 1994 and the inability of the government to meet its foreign debt payments. In 1994, Venezuela recorded Latin America's worst economic performance, with inflation registering more than 70 percent and the economy shrinking by 2 percent.

With oil revenues expected to be 20 percent lower in 1995 than in 1994, the government's budget deficit is headed toward 10 percent of Venezuela's GNP. With foreign interest fading, the nation's privatization program has virtually stopped. Foreign investors have lost interest in the country, citing exchange and price controls and the government's rough treatment of CANTV.

Little wonder that claiming Latin American economies successfully reformed is risky business. Like an addict of the drugs that grow so well there, the region has a history of reform and relapse. Nonetheless, there is some reason for optimism in the region. Brazil, the region's economic giant, does appear to have finally managed to grapple with its inflation problem, as evidenced by a stabilization plan complete with a new currency. Mexico, Argentina, Bolivia, and Panama have also managed to reduce inflation to single digits. Economic growth has also registered important gains in the region, with Peru leading the others at 12.5 percent in 1995.

Economic growth with low inflation has long eluded Latin America. The relative success can be attributed to reasonable macroeconomic stabilization policies. There also appears to be consensus on the importance of trade liberalization and privatization. Apart from some obvious exceptions, most countries in Latin America realized this years ago. For instance, Chile began reforming in the 1970s due in good part to the influence of the University of Chicago through reforms, students, and others. Colombia, for all its other problems, managed to keep in place reasonable macroeconomic policies.

There are exceptions to the relative inflation success stories. For one, Uruguay's 100 percent-plus inflation of the early 1990s is still 40 percent in the mid-1990s. Ecuador is only beginning to open up sectors like telecommunications and electricity. The long-term stability of Brazil's finances, and so its control of inflation, depends on deeper reforms.

Also important are the market liberalization reforms underway in the region. The bias toward autarchy, whereby emphasis was placed on high tariffs against imports and production mainly for the domestic market, has given way. Tariffs have been reduced; licenses and other restrictions have been abolished. Financial markets have also been opened up, interest-rate controls lifted, and directions of credit ended. Many countries have removed all restrictions on capital flows.

Privatization continues in the region. The sale of state firms has had two objectives. One is to reinforce macroeconomic stabilization; the other is to improve the economy's efficiency. As we have noted, in Chile and Mexico almost all state-owned firms have been sold. Even the slower privatizers in the region have made progress. Both Peru and Paraguay are making progress in privatization of their economies.

The net effect has been to encourage the flow of capital into the region. Commercial bank lending, popular in the turbulent 1970s, has given way to direct foreign investment and capital. Between 1990 and 1993, more than $170 billion net flowed in. About a third was foreign direct investment, which largely went into privatized assets; over half came from the issuance of private and public sector bonds.[6] Commercial loans made up a modest 5 percent. Much of this was capital that had fled earlier, and the bulk has gone to countries such as Mexico and Argentina. Latin America has become a big market for general investors in spite of the region's many problems.

These problems include a politicized and corrupt bureaucracy. Legal reform has hardly been handled adequately. Relations between local and central governments remain unclear and subject to confusion (e.g., in Brazil). A grinding poverty continues to constrain society, as does a skewed income distribution. The wealthiest fifth of the population of Mexico is 27 times richer than the poorest; in Argentina, 16 times richer. The private sector is still lagging in terms of job creation, and unemployment continues to grow across the region despite economic growth. In the countryside, poor farmers are short not only of land but of roads, bridges, and electricity. To this may be added the poor quality and inadequacy of elementary education.

How well Latin America manages to cope with its laundry list of problems will likely determine its future success. Effective government will be needed to help sort out the difficulties. The leading reformers, such as Chile, Argentina, and Mexico, have already started on the road to reform.

The rockiness of the road to such reforms is again illustrated in the case of Mexico and its efforts to privatize its economy. The illustration is provided in a decision that is viewed by American investors as a threat to their plans in the area of Mexican telecommunications.[7] Mexican government regulators continually approved a deal in which Telemex, the national telephone monopoly, would buy a 49 percent stake in the cable television subsidiary of Televisa, Mexico's largest media company. The $211 million sale would bring together two of Mexico's largest and most aggressive companies and would present a formidable challenge for American companies, such as MCI, GTE, and Sprint, which are planning to enter the Mexican telecommunications market when it opens to foreign investment in 1996. The Americans and their Mexican partners base their opposition on the claim that such a venture would create a new, government-sanctioned monopoly that would dominate the Mexican communications market.

The political dimensions of the problem are suggested by the fact the former president of the Mexican Government Commission on Competition, who took a hard line on monopolies and unfair competition by the country's large companies, left in December 1994. The Commission's new president was reported to be under strong pressure to approve the sale. Political pressure and the strength of Telemex unions reinforce the view that Televisa would be helped by such a merger, which would benefit both Mexican companies because Telemax always saw Televisa as a potential competitor in the telephone business. In effect, it is simply a way to preempt someone's entry into your market independently rather than by joining with them, as one analyst from Solomon Brothers observed of the venture. In any case, neither the privatization processes nor competition appear to benefit from such a merger in the country's telecommunication industry.

One can agree that the Latin American countries do indeed share a number of characteristics. Except for Brazil, they are all former colonies of Spain and gained independence from that country. Again except for Brazil, Spanish is the common language. Roman Catholicism is the common religion. Religion does appear to have had an important role in economic development in all societies. There is also the view held by many people in Latin America that chance dominates a person's life and that little can be done to improve their earthly circumstances. The Catholic and Spanish heritage underscores Latin America's penchant and preference for a hierarchical society.

It could be that these characteristics foster an attitude that tolerates the many durable political leaders that Latin America has known. For instance, in principle, Latin American countries do not believe a president should succeed himself, and most countries have constitutions which forbid it. Nevertheless, there are ways around such restrictions. Argentina's president has changed the rules and expects to get reelected. The same is true in Peru. Another way around the issue is to stage a political comeback, as in Venezuela and Uruguay.

The system lends itself easily to corruption. Some observers argue that such an arrangement is in good measure a part of the Latin American culture. They note that the Latin American countries were governed for 300 years by viceroys sent by Spain, usually as a reward for some favor done for the Spanish king. Many returned to Spain as rich men. Today it is almost an article of faith that any Latin American with any talent will acquire a fortune before leaving political office.

THE REGION'S EMERGING MARKETS

For all their problems, Latin American countries have achieved respectability among international investors. This is particularly true for managers of specialist emerging-markets funds, who control more than $100 billion in assets. Some of these managers have shifted their money from Southeast Asia to Latin America. The equity markets of Argentina, Brazil, Chile, and Mexico probably had a combined market capitalization of some $450 billion in 1994. The region's smaller markets, such as Colombia, Peru, and even Venezuela, have done well and continue to attract investors.

Further gains in Latin American markets can be expected. Except for Chile, most countries' stock markets are still small relative to their economies. According to figures reported in *The Economist*, the market value of all shares quoted on the Argentine stock market was only 13 percent of the country's GDP at the end of 1993 and Brazil's market capitalization was just 21 percent of its output compared with 98 percent for Chile's stock market, 313 percent for Malaysia's, and about the same for Hong Kong.[8] Another attraction, observers note, is that, except for Brazil, interest rates have fallen as inflation has been reduced; they have farther to fall, at least in nominal terms. Local investors may enter the market as buyers.

American fund managers are important players in the Latin American markets. It has helped that Latin shares have become easier to trade, as Mexican, Brazilian, and other equities have increasingly been bundled into American depository receipts (ADRs). There were 48 Latin ADR issues in 1993, up from one in 1989.[9]

Many pension funds and other institutions in the United States are limited to buying securities listed on U.S. stock exchanges there or, at least, denominated in dollars. *The Economist* reports that the 76 Mexican firms whose shares are available in ADR form account for 84 percent of Mexico's benchmark IPC share index and Argentina's 18 ADR issues account for 51 percent of that country's Merval index. Brazil lags behind, with only 7 ADRs, due to problems in adapting to American financial-reporting requirements.

A promising development is the so-called Mercosul, the beginning of a common market in South America, which thus far includes Argentina, Brazil, Paraguay, and Uruguay. Overall, intra-Latin trade has grown to 25 percent of the region's total trade, from 10 percent in the 1980s. Such a surge in trade has prompted business leaders in Latin America to push their governments to allow private companies to improve roads and communication. Copying the Mercosul system of express passport laws, the five nations of the Andean Pact—Bolivia, Colombia, Ecuador, Peru, and Venezuela—are expected to introduce a regional passport.[10]

Brazilian trade with Argentina is running at five times 1990 levels. In 1995, Brazil was reviewing 14 proposals from construction companies to link the two nations, the largest in South America. Moreover, Bolivia and Venezuela are exploring duty-free trade status with Mercosul, which would hasten the Andean Pact's move into what Brazilians are informally calling SAFTA—The South American Free Trade Association. In part, this is a reaction to the view that the United States will move slowly to extend NAFTA southward.

In fact, the Lehman Brothers' Latin American Growth Fund, a mutual fund formed shortly before Mexico devolved the peso, had in 1995 most of its investments in Brazil and Argentina and smaller amounts in Peru, Mexico, and Chile. Other funds (e.g., Chile Fund) are generally optimistic about opportunities in Latin America, in good measure because of developments such as Mercosul.

NOTES

1. See, for instance, F. Carroda-Bravo, *Oil, Money, and the Mexican Economy*, and *The Mexican Economy* (Boulder, CO: Westview Press, 1982); Robert E. Loomy, *Development Alternatives for Mexico* (New York: Praeger, 1982); Angus Maddison, *The Political Economy of Poverty, Equity, and Growth: Brazil and Mexico* (Oxford: Oxford University Press, 1992).

2. Calvin Sims, "Growls from Military Echo in Peru and Chile," *The New York Times*, Tuesday, June 20, 1995, p. A5. The crisis could not have come at a worse time. The country was in the middle of negotiations to join the North American Free Trade Organization.

3. Tim Golden, "Mexico Judge in Union Case Is Shot Dead," *The New York Times*, Wednesday, June 21, 1995, p. A7.

4. James Brooke, "Colombia Marvels at Drug Kingpin: A Chain-Saw Killer, Too?" *The New York Times*, Wednesday, June 21, 1995, p. A7.

5. The president of a consortium led by GTE Corporation of the United States, which runs Venezuela's CANTV phone company, B.E. Haddad, has been arrested once, has been called to testify before congressional committees 23 times, and has faced marches by union workers chanting, "Gringos out of CANTV." In 1994, the Venezuelan government

bureaucracy suddenly refused to allow his company to buy dollars, forcing it to default on millions of dollars in overseas loans. See James Brooke, "GTE Role in Venezuela Is Warning on Privatization," *The New York Times*, Wednesday, June 21, 1995, p. C1.

6. *The Economist*, Vol. 333, No. 7891, November 26, 1994, pp. 42–43.

7. Anthony De Palma, "Telmex Gains in Attempt to Buy Cable-System Stake," *The New York Times*, June 22, 1995, p. C4.

8. *The Economist*, Vol. 330, No. 7852, February 26, 1994, p. 84.

9. Ibid., p. 84.

10. James Brook, "More Open Latin Borders Mirror an Opening of Markets," *The New York Times*, Tuesday, July 4, 1995, p.C29.

5

East Asian Rim: Moving from State-Directed Capitalism?

COMPETING CAPITALISTS: JAPAN AND OTHERS

It was not too long ago that Japan served as an example for world businesspeoples. Japanese management, with its various examples of modernity and success of how to do things right, was the benchmark. Times do change. Sophisticated Japanese managers are now looking West, once again, at how western companies are dealing with various managerial and technological problems, including motivating people and tying together various far-flung world operations. The main elements of the Japanese model—consensus building (*nemawashi*) and shared decision making (*ringi*)—depend on close physical proximity and shared cultural values and simply do not lend themselves well to global operations.

It may be that southeast Asia, not Japan, is providing a model for the development of such countries as China and India.[1] Unlike Japan and South Korea, which have built up impressive industries and have made it difficult for foreigners to operate in their economies, the southeastern Asian countries of Singapore, Thailand, Malaysia, and Indonesia have welcomed foreigners. In fact, Singapore has an economy dominated by foreign-owned companies. The export industries of Thailand and Malaysia are controlled by foreign-owned enterprises.

Nonetheless, there is admiration in southeast Asia for the Japanese and South Korean government's sponsorship of such heavy industries as steel, shipbuilding, and automobiles. In fact, Malaysia and Indonesia have cultivated such industries as aircraft and automobiles, but with indifferent results. Thailand, on the other hand, has adopted the southeast Asian strategy of encouraging private direct foreign investment with positive results. In fact, all the southeast Asian countries have cultivated financial markets, unlike Japan and South Korea, where the focus was on bank lending and where such lending was monitored closely by government. The southeast Asian countries have also attracted to participate in their stock markets. As a result, firms in southeast Asia have had more access to financial resources and less debt problems than Japan and South Korea in their earlier industrialization. Malaya, Singapore, and Thailand have all registered economic growth rates of over 8 percent—far better than Japan or South Korea.[2]

Major countries in the area, such as India and China, have adopted elements of the southeast Asia model through very active stock markets and the encouragement of direct foreign investment. These developments are in marked contrast to events in the 1950s, 1960s, and 1970s, when both countries had inward-oriented strategies of development. Current world circumstances are different.

With the collapse of communism and the end of the cold war, open markets have assumed considerable importance on the world stage while political and ideological alliances and closed markets have slipped in importance to Western countries. Again, the importance of international capital markets and investors is underscored.

In some of the emerging markets in Asia, uncertainty over what will happen in 1997 when China takes control of the British colony has caused some investors to avoid Hong Kong, where the major stock index dropped 30 percent in dollar terms in recent years. Nevertheless, some investors view Hong Kong as a good investment because no one really knows what is going to happen when the colony becomes a part of China. In fact, in the view of some mutual fund investors with good knowledge of emerging markets, Malaysia and Thailand are simply overpriced. Other Asian markets, such as Pakistan and Sri Lanka, are not desirable due to past price run-ups in their markets. In short, there appear to be very few undiscovered markets in which investors can look forward to annual percentage returns in the upper teens.

It is, of course, not only the price of securities that tends to keep investors away. There are other practical matters, such as stock custody and stock settlement, that can keep investors away. Such concerns have left mutual fund managers reluctant to enter Hungary, India, Poland, and Russia, to name only the more obvious problem countries. Another concern is the lack of liquidity in a number of emerging markets, which prevents the sale of a stock when a mutual fund decides that a sale is appropriate.

IS JAPAN PROTECTIONIST?

Economists point out that on the surface Japan has a very open market. The formal economic evidence that the country is more protectionist than other countries is inconclusive. Accordingly, there is agreement that at least in manufactured goods the classic definition of protectionism, which entails government restrictions, suggests that Japan is not protectionist. In fact, Japan's tariffs are low and trade quotas are negligible. The average tariff rate is 3.3 percent, compared with 3.2 percent in the United States and 3.7 percent in the European Union. Japan imposes quotas on 66 categories of imports compared with hundreds in the United States and European Union. The country's imports rose 20 percent during the period 1990–1995, while its exports increased 30 percent.

If this is a correct picture, why does the Japanese market appear to be such a problem for foreigners? According to many foreigners seeking access to Japanese markets, the problems stem from informal barriers to trade. They point to a bureaucracy and volumes of regulations as well as to deep cultural traditions which shape all aspects of society, from the way the country organizes its economy to the way it runs its businesses and crafts its corporate goals. They also point out that these customs, often nebulous, effectively restrict foreign participation.

Since such restrictions are difficult to gauge, economists have resorted to market share data to suggest the magnitude of the problem with Japanese trade. For example, imports account for little more than 3 percent of Japan's overall economy, compared, for instance, with 8 percent for the United States. The difficulty with using market share data, of course, is that such data, though suggestive, are conclusive evidence protectionism.

Most European countries have a far tighter percentage of imports than the United States. This does not, however, mean that Europe is less restrictive than America. Nor does the American lack of interest in foreign movies and books suggest that the American government protects the movie and publishing industries.

It could be is more accurate to argue that while Japan is not as closed as some people believe nor as open as others believe, the truth is probably somewhere in between. Many economists believe that the Japanese system does not so much discriminate against foreigners as against outsiders, whether Japanese or foreign. This relates to the Japanese world of *keiretsu*, tightly knit alliances that tie the country's manufacturers to suppliers and distributors or to other companies in different markets. To foreigners, these alliances appear to engage in collusive behavior. To the Japanese, such arrangements represent collectivism or cooperation. Unlike their foreign counterparts, Japanese firms appear to place less emphasis on costs and more emphasis on relationships. Japanese firms like to have long-standing contracts with suppliers and to be absolutely sure that the suppliers are dependable. As a result, the outsider is faced with a significant barrier. The foreign firms that have established themselves as insiders appear satisfied with the Japanese system.[3]

Nevertheless, the American government is pursuing various initiatives for freer markets in Japan. In 1995, the Clinton Administration sought punitive trade sanctions to achieve its goals in Japan. At immediate issue in 1995 were the auto and auto parts markets. The goal, however, is not just sales but dismantling the system that Japan has built up since World War II and even earlier. The Clinton Administration efforts collided with three realities of economic diplomacy with Japan, which have changed very little since President Nixon declared in the early 1970s that the trade deficit with Japan, then a fraction of its 1995 level, had reached intolerable proportions.[4]

The first reality is that while the American government aimed for an accord that would awake the world's second largest economy and strike fear into the hearts of Asian countries tempted to imitate the Japanese model, what the Administration got was an agreement that simply expands the number of garages and mechanics who are permitted to make repairs for car inspections in Japan and that pressures Toyota dealers into thinking about putting American cars on their premises.

The second reality is that equal access to Japan's markets is a very subjective issue. According to the automobile arrangement, the American expectation is that by the end of the 20th century, more than 1,000 Japanese showrooms will be open to American automobile manufacturers. Japanese officials consider this a major advance, but one that they say will fall apart if the American Big Three automobile producers fail to invest heavily in some of the world's most expensive car dealerships in Japan.

The third reality is that broader political alliances still are predominant. In effect, the Clinton Administration, presumably the most export-focused in decades, decided that it was not worth risking its most important relationship in the Pacific for the extra concessions that might have been gained. The Japanese view the supposed benchmarks as vague because they did not agree to specific targets, a point which the Japanese view as an enormous victory. In effect, after two years of arduous and often bitter negotiations over the automobile trade, the United States and Japan have ended up as they started out—assuming an agreement over which they do not agree.

JAPAN'S MODEL IN HISTORIC PERSPECTIVE

It is possible to argue that the United States has only itself to blame for creating a troublesome Japan.[5] Accordingly, every important component of the Japanese sociopolitical and economic organization was put in place by the end of the American occupation in 1952. Much of the assembling was done with aid and encouragement from the American occupation authorities. For instance, Japan's Ministry of International Trade and Industry was already in operation at the end of the war in 1945.

Japan's priority production for cars, steel, and ships was in place in 1947. The country would achieve by diplomatic and economic effort what it failed to achieve through its nationalist international adventures. At the same time, Japan's security and foreign policy would be left to the United States. This is, in effect, the arrangement that was put together by Shigeru Yoshida, the Prime Minister who led the prewar political elite back to power in 1948, and General Douglas MacArthur, who led the occupation.

The results of these efforts on the world scene are clear. Japan's model is an example of state-directed capitalism. Along with South Korea and Taiwan, Japan has placed restraints on free markets and/or shaped them in ways to achieve and promote its development. These countries have restrained imports in order to develop domestic industries. They have relied on industrial policy to target certain industries for economic development.

Whatever the influence of the postwar years in constructing Japan's model, the elements of the model and its prototype were already in place many years before. In fact, it became clear to the Japanese as early as the mid-19th century that Japan either had to create a modern industrial state or become another market for

American and European goods. The Japanese decided for the creation of a modern state based on the Western model. Within a relatively short time, Japan had achieved its goal.

Insight into this remarkable transformation is gained by dividing Japan's development into three major periods: the Meiji Period, from 1868 to 1913; the interwar years, from 1914 to 1945; and the post-World War II years. A common characteristic of all three periods is the dominant role of the Japanese government in promoting and stimulating the processes of transformation.

The Meiji period marks the beginning of Japan as a modern industrial state. In the early years of the period, Japan made every effort to acquire the techniques, skills, and whatever else was necessary to acquire Western knowledge. This included pilot projects, foreign engineers and technicians, and sending abroad its people to acquire the necessary and desired skills. Everything possible was done to adapt Western technology and knowledge to Japanese conditions.

In all of these efforts, the Japanese government was a major player. Not only were major industries such as communication and transportation nationalized by the end of the 19th century, the Japanese government also built and operated shipyards, factories, and steel and iron plants. The government also devoted considerable resources to providing financial and technical assistance to private industry.

Japan's fiscal and tax policies were calculated to promote capital formation. Proceeds from tax collection and sales of land provided resources which went into the building of roads and educational facilities. Military needs were not disregarded, and considerable resources went into the building of military facilities.

Private enterprise also flourished and developed during the Meiji period. Among the new developments during these years was the displacement of the warrior caste, or *samurai*, which had dominated the country for centuries. Equally important is the fact that many of the *samurai*, as they were integrated into the general society, also went into business, thereby providing an elite upper-class element which made business ventures respectful and prestigious. This development is in marked contrast to the experience in many other developing countries, where the business groups were drawn from the lower strata of society, including immigrants.

The Meiji period ushered in a specifically Japanese form of business concentration or combines, called *zaibatsu*—literally, "financial powers." Each combine consisted of 20 to 30 firms, all concentrated around a large bank. These major firms represented each of the important industrial sectors in the economy. The *zaibatsu* brilliantly exploited great opportunities during the Meiji period, when the social and economic hold of feudal *daimyo* (noble) and *samurai* (knight) classes were broken. Mitsubishi, Mitsui, Samitomo, and Yasuda, known as Fuji, are examples of these old-line Japanese companies.

Through an interlocking, deliberately loose network of directorships and cross-investment more complicated than any Byzantine arrangement, these conglomerates controlled much of the country's economic activity. For the most part, the *zaibatsu* combines were larger than most U.S. companies and were under the control and management of a few family dynasties. For instance, the Mitsui combine employed 1,800,000 workers before World War II, and Mitsubishi employed 1,000,000 workers. The close arrangements between the *zaibatsu* and the Japanese government were such that the latter served to promote and penetrate markets for the *zaibatsu* through various means, including military force.

In the turbulent period between the two world wars, Japan was wracked by various insurrections, which tried to redress the social injustices in the country through force and assassination.[6] The Japanese have a special name for such legitimized criminal action: It is *grkokujo* (insubordination), a term first used in the 15th century when rebellion was rampant on every level, with provincial lords refusing to obey the *shogun* (a sort of generalissimo and de facto ruler in feudal Japan), who in turn ignored the orders of the emperor. With the reign of Meiji, the emperor of Japan had for centuries been little more than a figurehead, a puppet of the *shogun*.

The interwar tide of democracy, socialism, and communism that swept through Europe also had a dramatic impact on the young people of Japan, and they too raised the banner of change. Political parties had emerged, and a universal manhood suffrage bill was passed in 1924. These events, however, caught Japan unprepared to deal with the onrush of political, economic, and social events and changes. Many Japanese looked upon politics as a game to make easy money, and there were many scandals. Charges of bribery and corruption resulted in mob brawls on the floor of the Diet.

Economic, political, and social changes forced serious population shifts into the cities, where hundreds of thousands were out of work. For the first time in Japanese history, farmers close to starvation made organized attempts to protest their difficult circumstances. The net result was to produce a wave of reaction, both left-wing and right-wing nationalist varieties, with predictable results. This sad and catastrophic tale is well documented by such authors as John Toland.[7] Japan slipped toward war and conquest, which culminated in its defeat and occupation in 1945.

One of the experiments of Americans after World War II was the redemption of occupied Japan. Under the benign sponsorship of that paradoxical conservative, Army General Douglas MacArthur, moderates, liberals, leftists, and Marxists set out to remake a nation.

Their model was not specifically the social, economic, and political democracy in America. The institutions in the United States provided inspiration, but the reformers tried to improve on imperfect American practices. The docile Japanese apparently provided ideally malleable human material and surface economic and social structures had been cleared by the war—leaving skills and literacy as a foundation upon which to build. For the bemused Japanese determined to be in the front line of world powers ever since the Meiji period or Restoration in 1868 ended feudalism, the goal again seemed achievable.

Aside from inherent Japanese energy and ambition, certain specific results of the postwar experiment shaped the present Japanese model. These include the "democratic" constitution, which, among other provisions, deprived the emperor of divinity invented by the Meiji. Restoration renounced war as an instrument of national policy, redistributed large landholdings to their tillers, theoretically made access to education easier while weakening the ruling elite's monopoly of power, and broke up the *zaibatsu*, the great cartels which controlled the Japanese economy.

The country's success since 1945 has apparently stimulated the Japanese model to reacquire some of its earlier features. Thus the emperor's image is being cautiously refurbished. Japanese military power will unquestionably increase in the future. Only the land tenure system remains largely untouched. Education is, once again, virtually being monopolized by the elite—if it was ever otherwise. That elite again exercises tremendous power, and the *zaibatsu* are moving gradually—almost subterraneously, but implacably—toward significant influence in the economy and in politics. Because they control aggressive Japanese trading companies, they are the spearhead of Japan's economic penetration abroad. The new Japanese postwar model may remarkably resemble the old model revived.

Japan's new postwar constitution and subsequent laws dissolved the *zaibatsu* into a number of independent enterprises.[8] Antitrust laws molded after the U.S. Sherman and Clayton Acts were imposed on the Japanese. Later, however, the Japanese government enacted various laws to exempt certain industries from antitrust legislation. Japanese antimonopoly laws permit the development of cartels and other forms of business combinations to a far greater extent than is permitted by U.S. antitrust laws.

As before the war, the Japanese government continues to play a significant role in the country's economy. Apart from the usual instruments of intervention, such as government grants, subsidies, and low-interest loans, the Japanese government continues to maintain a close working relationship with the business community. There is apparently joint discussion and decision between government and business on investment projects and policies. Again the country's economy is but a reflection of its culture and historic factors, a number of which we have noted in this chapter.

For instance, Japan's industrial groups have no counterpart in other countries. Japan has the largest banks in the world, as well as a significant number of the world's largest corporations. These industrial groups are called the *keiretsu* and are of two types—vertical and horizontal.[9] The horizontal type consists of a family of corporations numbering many industries and centered around a bank. There are interlocking directorates in each *keiretsu*, and associated industries can own stock in each other. Bank loans to members are made at favorable interest rates and other terms.

The vertical type of *keiretsu* consists of an industrial group and its subsidiaries. Thus members can own shares of each other's firms and exchange information, including conducting and executing common strategies. The Japanese automobile industry provides a good example of such an operation (the industry has close ties with all its suppliers).

Another type of business organization in Japan is the *sogo shosha*, or trading company. There are about a half dozen such organizations, and they are among the largest enterprises in the world. They provide various services to their members, including procuring raw materials, distributing products, financing, exporting, and importing. Much of the country's foreign trade is conducted by these trading companies.

Japan's Ministry of International Trade and Industry (MITI) is probably the country's most powerful and influential bureaucracy. Its function is to provide guidance to the country's industries. This includes serious suggestions and recommendations regarding Japan's development. The Ministry is responsible for the flow of funds to favored industries as well as for allocating licenses and patents and for deciding which firms will receive them. The Ministry is also empowered to suspend antitrust laws, form cartels to aid industries, and encourage and develop particular industries. In fact, very little of anything in terms of economic activity can be undertaken in Japan without notification and authorization of the Ministry's bureaucrats.[10]

An appraisal of Japanese efforts in crafting successful policies to promote Japan's domestic and world trade leaves room for doubt. It is true that the country's interlocking relationship of business in the *keiretsu* facilitates the formation and execution of policies to promote trade interests probably better than, for instance, in the United States. The fact is that such efforts by Japan are also crowned by serious failure, as demonstrated in Japan's attempts to promote a civilian air transportation industry. Such inward-looking trade strategy as Japan's, with its promotion and protection of domestic industries, has come at the expense of the Japanese consumers—at least in the short term.

Other weak and problem areas in Japan in the long and short term are (1) the troublesome banking system, (2) an aging population which will require significant increases in resources devoted to social services, and (3) serious shortcomings in the infrastructure as a result of urban growth. Whether the young generation of Japanese is willing to continue the sacrifices required to stay the course of their parents remains an open question. The young generation appear more self-centered and less interested in making such sacrifices.[11]

OTHER ASIAN EXAMPLES: VIETNAM, KOREA, TAIWAN, AND INDIA

None of these issues and problems have deterred the Japanese from pushing their model elsewhere in Asia. Consider the example of Vietnam. Due to the American embargo on trade, which was lifted in 1994, Vietnam is the first economy to reach the point of takeoff without help from the West. Most of its investment comes from Taiwan, Japan, and Hong Kong. Most of its trade is with Asia. Japan alone provides fully half the aid that Vietnam gets from foreign governments.[12]

By mid-1995, Japan had a team of academics and officials in Vietnam to advise the Vietnamese on what sort of economy Vietnam should have: What should go into its next five-year plan, and how should the Vietnamese design their industrial policy and financial system? Japanese interest is understandable. Vietnam has a work force that is as cheap as Japan's is costly and aging. With an eye on developments in China, Japan apparently hopes to find an ally in traditionally anti-Chinese Vietnam. There is the added incentive of Japan's concern over the security of its oil supplies and tankers from Arab states which pass near Vietnam. Last, but certainly not least, is Japan's hopes to celebrate its new affinity with the rest of Asia, and its new self-confidence.

Japanese experts argue that Japan wants to share the knowledge gleaned from Japan's miraculous development, especially with Vietnam and other emerging markets in Asia. After all, they argue, the Vietnamese, like the Japanese, have been influenced by Confucius and value education, discipline, and strong government. There is a rich tradition, in their view, that underpins Asia's postwar success, and that Asians, including the Japanese, should take pride in. There is no need for Asians to conform to American rules. Given the demonstrated success of the Japanese model, there is every reason to believe that Japan should help lead a sort of Asian renaissance. In their view, Asia is no longer a place for Westerners to civilize and convert; its prosperity has revived Asia's independent dignity.

The Japanese experts, in particular, take exception to the criticism leveled at Japan's model by the World Bank and IMF, which they see as propagandists for the American model and the dominant goals of privatization, markets, and private stability. Such goals, if completely adopted by Asian emerging economies such as Vietnam, will hurt economic growth, undermine popular support for reform, create unemployment, and lead to a loss of government income that privatization might bring. The experts argue that strong state leadership is especially necessary in a country like Vietnam, where market forces are too rudimentary to be trusted.

Given Asian experience with Japan's "co-prosperity sphere" of the 1930s and early 1940s, it is not clear how receptive the Vietnamese and others will be to Japanese advice and their model. After all, the interventionist Japanese model was easier to follow in the 1960s than in the 1990s, since the industrialized Western countries are less likely to look with favor on trade protection. Moreover, the Vietnamese, in particular, are more likely to follow the American model and advice, with its emphasis on the development of equity and bond markets. The cash and development programs pushed by the Japanese may matter more to Japan than Vietnam.

Nonetheless, Vietnam has a long road to travel before it reaches its destination as a viable market economy attractive to most foreign investors. Plans for a stock exchange in Ho Chi Minh City (Saigon) by mid-1995 have been put off twice. The banking system is primitive—checks are virtually unknown. State-owned enterprises, which produced 43 percent of the GDP in 1994, are very weak, and more than a third are money-losing enterprises. The country's infrastructure of roads, rail, telecommunications, power, and outpost lie well behind Asian neighbors. The Vietnamese legal system leaves much to be desired. Vietnam in 1995 was still a very bureaucratic and complicated country.

Even so, with the normalization of relations between the United States and Vietnam, both nations expect an increase in American investment in Vietnam. The fact is that Vietnam has more than 73 million people—fewer than Germany, but more than Great Britain or France. Some investors see a low-wage source for manufacturing operations. Consumer-products companies hope for a potentially large market, and big energy companies are interested in Vietnam's oil and gas potential. By 1995, more than 50 countries with more than 1,200 investment licenses worth $14 billion were in Vietnam. In the decade 1985–1995, Taiwan—followed closely by investors from Hong Kong, Singapore, South Korea, and Japan—led the investment flow into Vietnam. Within six months in 1995, Japan has emerged as Vietnam's biggest foreign investor, with 30 projects valued at $754 million, more than a fifth of the $3.6 billion worth approved in the first half of 1995.

It is interesting that American investors, within six months in 1995, won approval for 11 projects worth $295 million. This places the United States in fifth place in terms of investments in Vietnam. The reasons given by the Vietnamese for favoring American participation in their economy provide useful insights. According to one report, the Vietnamese believe that Americans are sincere when they enter into a joint venture, and that American business has certain standards of conduct and is more responsible. They know Americans treat employees well.[13]

The other East Asian countries (in addition to Japan) usually labeled as Pacific Rim countries are South Korea, Taiwan, Singapore, and Hong Kong. All of them have several characteristics in common with Japan. Except for Japan, all have been created following World War II, and they are all resource poor, as is Japan. They all stress the important role for government in creating, promoting, and executing industrial development and national prosperity. They all, presumably, also share a commitment to free markets while pushing for state assistance to industry. In the cases of South Korea and Taiwan, both use economic planning that is linked to export development.

The South Korean example is a good one to illustrate the development of state-directed capitalism in Asia. In South Korea, a very close connection developed between the Korean government, its banks, and the *chaebol*, which are family-owned conglomerates similar to the prewar Japanese *zaibatsu*.[14] These family-owned conglomerates began in the early postwar period as small enterprises and subsequently expanded into conglomerates by cross-investments. Essentially, member firms of a *chaebol* invest in stocks to acquire new companies. They then use the increase in capital gained to borrow from banks at low interest rates. In effect, the Korean government subsidizes these family-owned organizations by government-supported bank loans that carry low interest rates with long maturity and, in effect, are nondefaultible because of government backing. South Korean banks, although state owned until the early 1970s and now privately owned, are still under government control in terms of their lending policies.

In Taiwan the influence of government is strong and active in economic affairs. The government is able to influence the country's industrial policy through state-owned banks, which allocate credit on the basis of priorities the government establishes for industries. The government has also taken direct responsibility for accelerating technology development and its application to industry.

India is another example of an Asian state-directed economy moving to increase the role of prices, markets, and private investment. Foreign investment in 1995 increased significantly, amounting to $700 million in the first four months compared to only $950 million for all of 1994. Competition among the country's states has been encouraged by India's liberalization reform program of 1991. The reform program cut back severely on centralized industrial controls, leaving the country's constituent states free to deal directly with investors. In fact, the state governments are now marketing themselves as attractive places for private investors in spite of some muttering in the grass roots about the abandonment of Marxist beliefs.

India has undertaken an ambitious program for reform and development of capital markets—far-reaching program of financial sector reforms, including adoption of internationally accepted prudential norms, interest rate liberalization, revamping of bank supervision, and encouragement of new private banks. At the same time, India has put in place a sustained effort toward macroeconomic stabilization. In fact, the primary issues in the country's stock market have more than tripled between 1991–92 and 1993–94.

NOTES

1. "Asia's Competing Capitalisms," *The Economist*, June 24, 1995, Vol. 335, No. 7920, pp. 16–17.

2. Ibid., p. 17.

3. There is also a very promising mail order business thriving between the United States and Japan. See Shuy and WuDunn, "Japanese Do Buy American: By Mail and a Lot Cheaper," *The New York Times*, Monday, July 3, 1995, p. A1.

4. Dave E. Sanger, "At the End, U.S. Blunted Its Big Stick," *The New York Times*, Friday, June 30, 1995, p. C5.

5. Patrick Smith, "The Irresponsible Super Power," *The New York Times*, Saturday, July 1, 1995, p. 15.

6. See, for instance, John Toland, *The Rising Sun: The Decline and Fall of the Japanese Empire, 1936–1945* (New York: Random House, 1970), pp. 5ff.

7. Ibid.

8. Corwin Edwards, "The Dissolution of Zaibatsu Continues," *Pacific Affairs*, September, 1946, pp. 8–24.

9. Ibid.

10. Some idea of the power and authority of Japan's MITI is suggested in that the equivalent U.S. organization would include the Departments of Commerce and Energy, the Office of the U.S. Trade Administration, the Export-Import Bank, the Small Business Administration, the National Science Foundation, the Overseas Private Investment Corporation, the Environmental Protection Agency, and parts of the Departments of Commerce and Justice. See, for instance, the discussion of MITI and Japan's industrial policies in Martin C. Schnitzer, *Comparative Economic Systems*, 6th ed. (Cincinnati, Ohio: South-Western Publishing Co., 1994), pp. 124–31. A good insight into Japan's sociopolitical and socioeconomic structure is provided in Congress of the U.S. Joint Economic Committee, *Japan's Economic Challenge* (Washington, DC: U.S. Government Printing Office, 1991); Shintaro Ishihara, *The Japan That Can Say No: Why Japan Will Be*

First among Equals (New York: Simon & Schuster, 1991); Charles Turner, *Japan's Dynamic Efficiency with Global Economy* (Boulder, CO: Westview Press, 1991).

11.   See, for instance, Marvin Centron and Owen Davies, *Crystal Globe: The Haves and Have-Nots of the New World Order* (New York: St. Martin's Press, 1992), Chapter 11.

12.   "The Struggle for Vietnam's Soul," *The Economist*, July 24, 1995, Vol. 335, No. 7920, pp. 33–34.

13.   See Edward A. Gargan, "For U.S. Business, a Hard Road to Vietnam," *The New York Times*, Friday, July 14, 1995, pp. C1 and C5.

14.   For a discussion of the South Korean model and the important role of the *chaebol*, see Martin C. Schnitzer, *Comparative Economic Systems*, 6th ed. (Cincinnati, OH: South-Western Publishing Co., 1994), pp. 73–76.   Unlike Japan's *keiretsu*, the *chaebols* do not have a bank at their core but a trading company.   Hyundai is an example of a Korean *chaebol*.

6

Africa and Emerging Markets: A Legacy of Colonialism

FROM COLONIALISM TO INDEPENDENCE: A DIFFICULT ROAD

North Africa, as a part of the Mediterranean basin, has been associated with Europe from the earliest period of human history. The expansion of Islam, however, divided the Mediterranean Sea into two distinct culture regions. In the 19th century, Europeans expanded their interest in African territories. The whole continent, with only two exceptions (Liberia and Ethiopia), was soon divided between various European states.

The Spanish and Portuguese established the earliest colonies in Africa. Spain claimed the Canary Islands in 1497, and Portugal established colonies on the Indian (Mozambique) and the Atlantic (Angola) coasts in 1505 and 1576, respectively. French interests on Madascar date from about 1642. The British developed a trading plantation in Sierra Leone in about 1737, and the Spanish added the island of Fernando Po (off the Cameroons) in about 1797. The British established colonies at Cape Town (1814), Gambia (1816), and Natal (1842). Spain added outposts along the Atlantic coast at Guinea (Rio Muni) and Ifnian in 1842 and 1860. France claimed Somaliland and Algiers in 1802 and 1830.

Prompted by industrialization in Europe and the consequent requirement for raw materials as well as overseas markets, the race for colonies began in earnest. Improvements in transportation, particularly railroads, opened up possibilities for profitable ventures and settlement in the African interior. By 1870, the processes of European civilization gained momentum. The British gained control of Egypt in 1882, Anglo-Egyptian Sudan in 1989, British East Africa in 1895, Nyasaland in 1891, Rhodesia in 1889, and Bechuanaland in 1885. The French colonies included Tunisia (1881), the Ivory Coast (1893), French Equatorial Africa (1885–1895), French West Africa (1911), and Morocco (1911).

Belgium interests in the Congo dated from the 1880s, although the Belgian Congo did not become an official colony until 1908. Germany acquired Togoland and South West Africa in 1884 and German East Africa in 1890. Italy was a latecomer to African colonization, taking Italian Somaliland in 1889, Eritrea in 1890, and Libya in 1912.

Thus the European countries shared the division of African territory. Their African colonies were governed by administration sent from London, Paris, Berlin, Rome, Madrid, Brussels, and Lisbon. The entire administrative, bureaucratic, and military answered to their respective capitals in Europe. Economic activity was for the most part in control of Europeans or Asians. For the native Africans, there was little room in the colonial administration or in the economy. When these former colonies finally gained independence in the years following World War II and the foreign bureaucrats and experts returned to their home countries, a vacuum was created. Into this vacuum came a singularly unprepared native African personnel with little if any training in government and rudimentary technical skills.

To make matters worse, African nationalism drove out the Indian and Chinese merchants from some African countries. Economic, political, and social instability soon followed in many newly independent African countries. All too frequently what native leadership was available fell wide of the mark of even minimal requirements and showed more interest in gaining and holding political power. Since the 1960s, more than 70 leaders in African countries have been deposed by assassinations, purges, or military coups.

The results of African colonial and postcolonial experience are predictable.[1] Poverty, corruption, disease, religious fanaticism, tribal warfare, and civil war have scarred the continent for much of the postindependence years. Much the same was also true during the colonial period, though the colonial authorities managed to keep a lid on at least some of the disturbances in their respective African colonies.

GROWING IMPORTANCE OF POSTAPARTHEID SOUTH AFRICA

A turning point in Africa's future has taken place with the end of apartheid in South Africa. The end of apartheid is helping to revitalize the continent. Economists are now underscoring that South Africa will likely play an important, if not dominant, role in the continent's future development. With apartheid dead, South Africa's pent-up entrepreneurial energy is exploding all over Africa.[2] The country's industries are building railroads in Zaire, developing mines in Ghana, building hotels in Kenya, and providing enough jet aircraft and telephone lines to make a real difference in Africa's hitherto sagging fortunes. In fact, South Africa's exports to the rest of the continent were up 50 percent in 1993–1994 to nearly $2.5 billion, and imports tripled to $664 million from $220 million. South Africa's expanding presence is displacing much of the economic and cultural influence long exerted by France and the United States. One can almost rest assured that South Africa's political influence may soon follow its trade.

Many people would find it ironic that postapartheid South Africa's impact on the rest of the continent is more economic than political. When President Nelson Mandela took power in 1994, some of his foreign supporters expected him to become a bold force for political change, denouncing human rights abuses and promoting democratic movements elsewhere in Africa. Instead, he has kept a low profile, making it clear that South Africa will not play political tutor to the rest of Africa—at least not in the immediate future.

This is in marked contrast to South Africa's businesspeople who appear to be making their work all over the continent. Moreover, most African countries appear to welcome their efforts. Several African governments have begun to advertise their World Bank-mandated privatization of state companies in South African newspapers, expecting to entice bidders. The fact that South Africans are interested in local partners and desire to build joint ventures on the continent has raised suspicion on the part of some former colonial powers.

France, for instance, has maintained the closest and strongest ties to Africa. South African success in several markets has prompted French observers to warn of the increasingly aggressive financial, industrial, and commercial competition, in particular by Anglo-Saxons and Japanese in league with South African firms. In particular, the observers note South Africa's successful ventures in Zaire, formerly ruled by Belgium. As Western firms have withdrawn from Zaire because of corruption and, in general, difficulty in doing business there, South African concerns have moved in, seeing its mineral wealth, need for roads and railways, as well as development of hydroelectric power. Many Africans are beginning to see that they are not going to get much economic and financial assistance from Paris, Washington, or London.

South Africa continues to be faced with serious problems that may turn off potential investors. There is, for instance, a culture of resistance which may constitute a continuing problem.[3] The African National Congress, during the apartheid period, urged residents of Soweto and other black townships to stop paying their rent, electricity, and water bills. These boycotts were a powerful weapon against the apartheid government, eventually crippling and bankrupting local authorities. What the African National Congress created has now come to haunt the new administration. Put simply, people are not paying their bills. This leaves the government without the resources to make improvements which people insist on before they will pay their bills.

The government has resorted to, among other things, an advertising campaign about the virtues of paying one's bills, promoting such payment as a form of patriotism. The apartheid government tried to break the boycotts by evicting families, making threats, and arresting boycott activists, to no avail. Some idea of how effective the new government's policy has been is suggested by a return to cutting off services to delinquents. Apparently there is now agreement that there has to be a price attached to not paying. There is little talk about rebuilding South Africa among the disgruntled customers lining up to pay their bills.

Another serious problem in South Africa deals with land issues and, in effect, property rights. Black South Africans were driven from their homes and land between 1913 and 1989.[4] *The Economist* points out that as white farms swelled in size, black ones became ever more crowded and overgrazed. By 1970, the average size of a white farm was 988 hectares (2,470 acres)—at a time when the average in the United States and Canada was 161 hectares—but the average black farm had only 1 hectare.

Government land reform now envisions first a restoration to original owners or their heirs. Second, the goal is to redistribute to the black majority a total of 30 percent of the country's arable land. Third, the idea is to modernize tenure by giving tenant farmers who have lived on a white farm for more than a generation the right to buy land. All the claims are made against the state, not the owner; the court can then compel the government to compensate the evicted person, either by buying the land, for which it must pay the owner a market rate, or by funding comparable land somewhere else. Anybody with a claim must take it to the newly created land-claims commission within the three years from the law's establishment.

The difficulties such reform poses are the potential open-ended bill that the government could run up buying back confiscated land. Government-held land is sold to pay for these reforms. When that money runs out, who should pay for the remainder of the land that will have to be bought? Banks will be required to help small farmers pay for more land, water, fertilizer, and so on.

The problem of involving banks in such a scheme is that the land being returned under the restitution program is, like other land across Africa, held communally and administered by the chief. Of course, banks are unwilling to treat communally held land as collateral for loans. Moreover, without security of ownership, farmers have little incentive to look after or invest in their land. The issue is further complicated by the fact that in traditional parts of Africa, the patriarchal inheritance system often means that, if a man has no sons, his land passes to his brother, not his wife. In a country where the women do most of the farm labor, that can leave a widow without any land at all. Little wonder that the agreement's land reform places considerable emphasis on land tenure matters and property rights.[5]

Another source of concern for the potential investor in South Africa are the 11 official national languages provided for in the new constitution.[6] None is constitutionally more equal than another. Members of parliament, for instance, have the right to speak in any of the 11 languages. Although translation of these languages for members is available for other members, it can mean listening to a debate without understanding a word. Supposedly, all official documents are available in all 11 languages; many are, in fact, printed in only four. How these efforts at multilingualism will improve communication among South Africans and foreigners remains to be seen.

DIFFERENT COUNTRIES, SIMILAR PROBLEMS FOR THE INVESTOR

In Kenya, President David Arap Moi is certain that his political opponents are working with foreign businesspeople to recolonize Kenya. Of course, President Moi does not tolerate opposition willingly. A one-party state has always suited him best. He vigorously opposed multiparty democracy and admits he only accepted it in 1991 as a result of pressure from the West.

Kenya and its government obviously leaves something to be desired by foreign investors. Even Great Britain, a traditional friend of Kenya, is exasperated with the government's behavior. By 1995, the World Bank had suspended $260 million earmarked for the country's infrastructure and may suspend another $100 million that had been going into energy. At the same time, Germany has halved its $60 million aid to Kenya, Denmark may cut its aid by $20 million, and Japan, the country's largest donor, has frozen $15 million in aid.

All of this is an attempt by the donor countries to put Kenya back on the reform track. The country's finance minister is willing to cooperate and push reform, including cuts in the budget deficit and civil service, the privatization of more state farms, and lifting of bans on certain food imports. The problem, of course, is how much support the finance minister will receive from his president.[7]

Another example is Nigeria, Africa's largest country. The country did not exist as a national entity. Its earlier centuries of existence were dominated by slave trade. It became a formal British colony in 1860 and was recognized by other European powers as a British enclave at the Berlin Conference of 1885.[8]

As with many other colonies, colonial rule was a mixed blessing. In Nigeria, Britain built railroads and other infrastructure. Trade and banking were run by companies chartered in Britain. Barclay's Bank ran the banking system, and the Royal Neger Company was responsible for crops for export. Rules, attitudes, and the British colonial administration, together with firms and churches, excluded Nigerians from participation in government and commerce.

After World War II, the British-Nigerian colonial relationship changed. More Nigerian participation in Nigeria's activities was encouraged. By 1960, when Nigeria achieved independence, the country had a bureaucracy that had some experience with government, and a small but expanding business class. The Nigerian government plays a dominant role in the country's enormous development. In fact, the government is the country's largest employer. It is responsible for the development of the national economic plans and setting of planning priorities. It grants subsidies and makes loans to various sectors of the economy and implements foreign trade policy.

Among the more important developments during the postcolonial period in Nigeria is the increase in the country's private sector.[9] For the most part, the increase took the form of foreign direct investment. The oil bonus of the 1970s provided a boost both to public and private enterprise. Nonetheless, the many private enterprises, due to their small size, find it difficult to acquire capital and technological expertise to make the transition to large-scale operations.

Similar to many other oil producers elsewhere in the world, the economy of Nigeria deteriorated badly during the 1980s. The drop in the world price of oil from $40 a barrel in 1980 to a low of $14 a barrel in 1987 administered a severe shock to Nigeria's economy. Oil continues to be Nigeria's primary cash resource. Nigeria derived 95 percent of its export revenue in 1991 and 1992 and 80 percent of its budget revenue from the sale of oil. As world oil prices increased in the late 1980s, so did Nigeria's economy.

Nigeria also incurred a considerable foreign debt during the 1980s, from $8.9 billion in 1980 to $36.1 billion in 1990, or from about 9 percent of GNP in 1980 to a startling 118 percent in 1990. Nigeria's experience with debt is similar to that of many Latin American countries, except that Nigeria is poorer. The expectations were that the oil revenue would continue to increase and thus facilitate repayment of debt. Unfortunately, the loans in Nigeria were not invested in profitable projects but were wasted in those of little value.

A growing population, more than 250 ethnic groups with different languages and customs, active tribal and religious rivalries, and less than 25 percent of the relevant age group (persons 15 to 22 years old) in secondary school or college provide Nigeria with an inventory of serious problems. To these problems may be added endemic corruption, including political corruption. Political instability serves to underscore these problems. Nigeria has been ruled more or less by the military since its independence from Great Britain in 1960. In general, Nigeria has a limited experience with democracy.

The sad fact is that Nigeria, richly endowed with oil and mineral wealth, should be one of Africa's most prosperous and successful countries but is not. Misrule, usually by generals, is an obvious fact of Nigerian political life. Secret trials, convictions, and worse are a continuing source of domestic rancor and international isolation. Intolerant of its critics, the regime of General Sani Abodia, which seized power in November 1993, has been notoriously tolerant of big-time drug traffickers. As a result, Nigeria has become a principal trans-shipment point for Asian heroin and Latin American cocaine en route to the United States. Because of this, Washington has ruled Nigeria ineligible for American assistance.

PROMOTING AFRICAN DEVELOPMENT: MISSION IMPOSSIBLE

Early in 1995, TransAfrica, an African-American human rights lobbying group prominent in earlier boycotts of South Africa, called for an international boycott of Nigerian oil to protest General Sani Abacha's repressive regime. TransAfrica had plenty of company, including United Nations Secretary General Boutras-Ghali and Pope John Paul II. Such criticism is not likely to encourage the private investor to take Nigeria seriously.

Unfortunately, the example of Nigeria is not unique in Africa. Direct foreign investment in Africa is so negligible, amounting to only 3 percent of global flows, that few of Africa's countries even bother to keep data on private investment. In fact, Africa is in such sad shape that it actually lurched backward at a time when poor countries elsewhere have sprung ahead. The total wealth of Africa in 1995, with twice the population of the United States, is a little more than that of Belgium.

The former French colonies have not fared better in extricating themselves from the ruins of colonialism. The late President Charles de Gaulle, who mounted the resistance of "Free France" from the former French colonies, was fond of saying that without Africa there would be no France. Indeed, President Jacques

Chiroc's 1995 trip to Africa was both reaffirmation of his Gaullist roots and a reminder that the links that Paris still maintains with Africa are nearly all that stands between France and a decidedly more humble international stature.

President Chiroc inherited President DeGaulle's conservative ideology and thus visited Africa, a continent that has been forgotten by its former colonizers. The fact is that France can usually count on support from its former African colonies for its various positions taken in the United Nations. In the former French colonies, there is also an opportunity to provide French firms with contracts unfavorable considerations.

The nostalgia of the African French colonial elites for a simpler Gaullist past has long been cultivated by Chiroc and others. Paris, they say, was long the guarantor of stability for a colonial operation that paid little attention to democracy. President Chiroc has made a point that democracy is a luxury that Africa can ill afford. He has criticized the growing power of the World Bank and International Monetary Fund, often seen as American surrogates, in shaping the destinies of France's former possessions to the detriment of lucrative relationships that still bind many former colonies in Africa to France.

On the other hand, President Chiroc's Prime Minister Alain Juppé has put forth his own analysis, denouncing the criminalization of Africa and the elite in power.[10] Juppé and others are arguing for radical reform of French assistance to Africa aimed at eliminating corruption and subjecting these countries to the same kind of aid criteria that apply elsewhere in the world. Other French advisors obviously disagree. One of Chiroc's closest advisors, Jacques Foccart, who accompanied Chiroc to Africa, is widely considered the architect of France's traditional system of wielding control in Africa through parallel diplomacy, which uses such channels of contact as secret transactions, and military assistance.[11]

Even America's contribution to the development of Africa, Liberia (one of the only two African countries not colonized by Europe), slipped into civil war in 1989. Colonized by former American slaves in the 19th century, today Liberia is carved up by several rival forces with warring fiefs. The wreckage of Liberia is devastating for the thousands of Liberians unable to return to their country for fear of being killed by any one of the rival forces in control of various parts of Liberia. They are refugees in neighboring countries, such as the Ivory Coast. The bloody ethnic wars still going on in 1995 in other parts of Africa, such as Angola, Sudan, Liberia, and Burundi, underscore the plight of the continent and its wretched refugee camps.

The failings which have handicapped Africa's efforts at reform and development are as much political as economic. Thus it is that foreign investors who might otherwise be attracted by Africa's relatively inexpensive labor are deterred by the hassle of dealing in countries where the rules of law are so weak that even simple contracts can be difficult to enforce.[12] Bribes to badly paid bureaucrats are a way of doing business. These bribes, for all practical purposes, constitute an informal welfare system. They also serve to break an obstructive bureaucracy and force firms to pay heavily for doing business in Africa. In fact, the World Bank and International Monetary Fund are reluctant to portray Africa as a loser for fear of scaring away potential investors. They delicately avoid mentioning the word corruption and never use that word in the same breath as the name of an individual country.

Even the continent's relatively best performing economies—English-speaking Ghana and two French-speaking neighbors, Burkina Faso and the Ivory Coast—underscore the legacy of colonialism and the fragmentation that the colonial powers encouraged.[13] This fragmentation is another stumbling block to development in Africa. These three countries are but a case in point. Together they form a natural economic unit whose market, with a total population of 40 million, would begin to make it inviting to foreign investors. Separately they are poor, small, and isolated markets in which the potential reward for outside investors often seems too small to justify the perceived risks of doing business in Africa.

Africa's failure to coalesce can be attributed in good measure to the arbitrary European imposition of borders in the 19th century. Many experienced analysts and frustrated businesspeople attribute the costly mistakes made by Africans and their foreign investors to the independence era, which began with Ghana's statehood in 1957.[14] They condemn the rapid transformation of many African countries into predatory states. Many of their governments have simply served to expropriate businesses and/or impose confiscatory taxes or demand bribes. The political will to make changes does not exist because agents of the state have grown used to using corruption to round out their personal budgets.

At the same time, the outside world has played an important role in continuing the fragmentation or Balkanization of the continent. Prominent here, according to some observers, are the World Bank and IMF. France is the most active of the European countries on the continent and the only former colonial power to have retained its grip on its one-time colonies. The World Bank and other lenders duplicate Africa's fragmentation and ultimately help perpetuate it by organizing their projects on a country-by-country basis.

Moreover, it is not only the selfishly defined interests of various ruling political elites reluctant to cede any portion of their sovereignty, it is (in the case of French-speaking Africa) France itself that is reluctant to encourage its former colonies to integrate with English-speaking countries. Much of France's objection to an integrated West Africa of 40 million is that such an economic giant would come to rival France's influence in the region. France worked to dismember Nigeria by actively supporting Biafran secessionists during Nigeria's civil war in the late 1960s. In support of such accusations, businesspeople in West Africa describe different actions by Paris in the region in 1995 aimed at limiting non-French interests in many spheres, be they those of English-speaking Africans or Westerners.

THE ISSUE OF ISLAM

Various campaigns in Africa to move against Muslim militants do not appear to have had much success or attraction to potential foreign investors. In Egypt, for instance, critics of the Muslim Brotherhood have long argued that its leaders have supplied financial and ideological support to an estimated 3,000 underground fighters, who have been battling the Egyptian government since 1992. Similar crackdowns against militant Islamic movements and figures have taken place in many of the North African countries. Egypt has accused the government of Sudan of supporting a failed plot to assassinate President Hosni Mubarak of Egypt in Ethiopia in June 1995.

Consider, for instance, the ongoing tragedy of the 1990s in Algeria. It is, in fact, a battleground where a militant political Islamic movement may seize power. Hundreds of leading figures in Algeria, including intellectuals, politicians (one of them a president), journalists, emancipated women, foreigners, and thousands of ordinary Algerians, have fallen victim to fundamentalist violence. Algeria is important because a militant political Islam will lead to violence.

Recent attempts to "rethink Islam" in a modern mode may not be any more successful than efforts to reform communism, which ultimately led to a dead end. This does not mean, of course, that Islamic revival is a useless exercise. Militant movements so much in the news see as their task mobilization for political action. Their common thread is hostility to the West. The antithesis to their efforts are those calling for integration of Islam with Western cultures. In this view, the task is to revitalize Muslim faith and intellectual culture.

Those experts arguing for revitalization of Islam tend to be highly critical of the past and present conditions of Islamic thought and contemporary Islamic societies, though not always by name.[15] Some people argue, in effect, that the Koran's spiritual transformative power over the hearts and minds of Muslims has been obscured. In their view, the spiritual essence of the covenant between God and people has been allowed to deteriorate into legal codes, rituals, and ideologies of domination in the interest of religions and political elites. Much of the early achievements of Islam have been abandoned long ago. Currently the various Islamic regimes suppress, control, and manipulate Islam simply to remain in power while Islamic opposition movements, contrary to their claims, actually secularize their societies. Their vocabulary of religious reference is without genuine religious vision. These critics underscore that the best place and prospects for the revival of Islamic culture are in the West, for the simple reason that no Muslim society permits independent intellectual criticism.

In effect, the revival of Islamic culture depends on a Muslim renaissance that would allow for a thinking of the hitherto unthought in Islam. This would require a revival of the philosophic, scientific, and humanistic culture of Islam's classical period and the assimilation of the industrial and information revolutions with their modern social, scientific, theological, and philosophical insights. This is nothing less than putting in place an intellectual apparatus essential to a critical formulation of an Islam modernity—an overwhelming task indeed, but if it is not undertaken and successful, Islam will be in a form that is communalist, separatist, and parochial.

It is not at all clear whether such a rational, ethical, and individualistic vision of Islam will satisfy those who respond to militant political Islamic movements.

It may, however, appeal to the few and perhaps to the Muslim populations of modernized industrial societies. The problem is that Islam can claim few such societies. More typical of Islamic societies are uprooted peoples deprived of such elementary rights as political participation, education, employment, and adequate health and housing facilities. Little wonder that such people are easy prey for militant political Islamic movements.

NOTES

1. For a useful discussion of Africa's problems, see World Bank, *Africa's Adjustment and Growth in the 1980s* (New York: Oxford University Press, 1989); David D. Simon, *Cities, Capital and Development: The African Experience* (Lymington, England: Belhaven Press, 1992); United Nations, *Maldevelopment of a Global Failure* (New York: United Nations Publications, 1990); United Nations, *Human Development Report 1992* (New York: Oxford University Press, 1992).

2. See, for instance, Howard W. French, "Out of South Africa, Progress," *The New York Times*, Thursday, July 6, 1995, pp. C1 and C5.

3. See Suzanne Daley, "In South Africa a Culture of Resistance Dies Hard," *The New York Times*, Wednesday, July 19, 1995, p. A3.

4. "Winning Back Their Land," *The Economist*, June 24, 1995, Vol. 335, No. 7920, pp. 37–38.

5. Some idea of how strong tradition is in African society is suggested in that even Nelson Mandela confessed in early 1995 that he had gained a freehold title to a piece of land near his home in the Transkei because he is on good terms with the chief, who also happens to be his nephew. See "Winning Back Their Land," *The Economist*, June 24, 1995, Vol. 335, No. 7920, p. 38.

6. "Surfing through the Languages," *The Economist*, June 24, 1995, Vol. 335, No. 7920, p. 38.

7. Such support does not appear to be forthcoming. Thus, in mid-1995, Mr. Moi pressed ahead with an $84 million international airport for his home town. See "Kenya: Into the Ark," *The Economist*, June 24, 1995, Vol. 335, No. 7920, p. 40.

8. See Gavin Williams, *Nigeria: Economy and Society* (London: Rex Collings, 1976).

9. Sayre P. Schatz, *Nigerian Capitalism* (Berkeley: University of California Press, 1977).

10. Howard W. French, "French President Affirms Ties to Africa," *The New York Times*, Saturday, July 22, 1995, p. A5.

11. Ibid., p. A5.

12. "Africa: A Flicker of Light," *The Economist*, March 5, 1994, Vol. 330. No. 7853, p. 24.

13. Howard W. French, "West Africans Find Prosperity Is Elusive: Region Seems Unable to Overcome Past," *The New York Times*, Sunday, April 9, 1995, p. A9.

14. Ibid.

15. See, for instance, Mohammed Arkoun, *Common Questions, Uncommon Answers* (translated and edited by Robert D. Lee) (Boulder, CO: Westview Press, 1994). See also Ira Milapidus, "Islam without Militance," *The New York Times Book Review*, August 21, 1994, pp. A9–10.

7

Debt Crisis Revisited

MEXICO AGAIN?

It would appear that the international debt crisis of the 1980s has been overcome.[1] There are, however, new worries which have emerged in the 1990s. The Mexican crisis in the 1990s underscores these concerns. The country's experience in the early 1990s suggests that although foreign capital can help developing countries grow faster, it leaves them less room to make mistakes.

Foreign investors are understandably nervous. After all, it was Mexico that triggered the third-world debt crisis in the early 1980s. Though the crisis in the 1990s contains lessons for policy makers in other emerging markets and economies, there are also lessons for international investors. The fact is that Mexico's recent debacle, as we have discussed elsewhere in this study, can be attributed to its current account deficit, which in 1994 reached 8 percent of GDP. This is even higher than it had been at the beginning of the 1980s debt crisis. Many other emerging economies in Latin America and Asia were also running large deficits in the early 1990s. This did not present a problem due to the inflow of private foreign capital. But Mexico's experience also suggests that private foreign investors can change their minds very quickly and capital can flow out.

A large current account deficit does not by itself mean a failed economy. Profitable investment opportunities in emerging markets will attract capital from more mature industrial economies in particular. If a country runs a capital surplus, it must by definition run a current account deficit. This is the way the adjustment process takes place. Thus the inflow of capital allows the emerging economies and countries to invest more than they save and so grow faster. If properly invested, a current account deficit should be no cause for concern.

In Mexico, as we noted, the problem was different from that of the early 1980s. In the early 1990s, the country's government budget was in balance. This indicates that the government was not the problem, but rather the current account deficit reflected private sector borrowing and spending. Moreover, private foreign investors were willing to finance the deficit, as judged by Mexico's build-up of significant foreign reserves.

The problem for Mexico was that its current account deficit was not sustainable. Although part of the deficit came about as a result of higher investment, a significant part also came from a decline in domestic savings and so higher consumption. Moreover, Mexico was also the recipient of so-called hot money. This was, in effect, speculative investment in equities or short-term deposits. It was not the more stable form of foreign direct investment. The net result was that Mexico was made vulnerable to the gyrations of investor confidence fueled in good measure by the country's perceived political instability. The rise in American interest rates at that time (1994–95) made investment in emerging markets less attractive. Funds moved out of Mexico as a consequence of the American interest rate rise. Mexico's problems were worsened by the government's inept devaluation of the peso in December 1994.

Important as Mexico's lessons are for private investors and policy makers, the prospects for emerging markets are good provided that emerging country governments continue their free market reforms and fiscal prudence. Emerging economies as a whole are still expected to grow twice as fast as the developed industrial countries into the next century.

In effect, private investors need not avoid investing in emerging markets. They should, however, do so in a cautious and discriminating manner with careful attention to the evidence. In particular, investors should pay attention to whether an emerging market country's deficit is being financed by long-term or speculative capital inflow, whether a widening deficit reflects rising investment or consumption, and whether the government is running a budget deficit.

THE 1970s AND 1980s WORLD DEBT ISSUE

The enormous foreign debt incurred by developing countries in the 1970s and 1980s threatened to damage economic growth seriously not only in the debtor countries but in the world economy in general. Steps were taken, and some were successful in mitigating the more serious consequences to the world economy.

Most experts agree that during that period, much of the borrowing, especially by developing countries, occurred to finance current consumption rather than investment. One consequence of such borrowing is that it does not generate income with which to defray interest and amortization charges, so future consumption must be sacrificed to meet these costs. Many countries have avoided these inevitable sacrifices by additional borrowing. The problems for these countries are thereby simply exacerbated. Eventually lines of credit are diminished, if not exhausted, and the country is forced to export more than it imports, using part of its export receipts to defray interest and amortization charges that were contracted in the past. As these resources are transferred abroad, the living standards in the country decline. The country will also restrict imports, with damaging effects on its economic growth as well as that of its trading partners.

The debt situation is particularly grave for small debtor countries. Usually their obligations are so great that they must pay annual interest and debt amortization to the extent that little foreign exchange is available to purchase essential imports.

The consequent undermining of economic growth and reduced living standards also undermine social and political instability. The chain of events set in motion by these circumstances is now all too familiar: Import restrictions necessitate a combination of devaluation, which produces adverse terms of trade; deflation, whose immediate effect may produce unemployment; and exchange and trade restrictions which produce resource misallocations that further reduce real revenue levels. Import restrictions, when they reduce the impact of capital goods, cast in doubt the country's ability to increase capital formation and employment.

The developed industrial countries also pay a price for developing country debt when their exports to debtor countries are curtailed as these countries restrict their imports. Moreover, the financial and banking stability in industrial countries is threatened as well. Large commercial banks in industrial countries are usually principal creditors for debtor countries. A default by any major debtor country or countries could cause a severe financial and banking crisis. It does not necessarily follow that a default that would impact on creditor banks would harm the economy at large. Deposit insurance and the ability to control banks (to provide the necessary liquidity by open market operations) and direct lending to banks could protect the remainder of the economy. This would, of course, have adverse effects on bank stockholders, who would suffer losses. Whether governments should step in to bail out creditor banks for their follies in making uncollectible loans is a matter of debate.

During the 1970s and 1980s, major defaults were avoided, although suspension of interest payments did occur. It may be tempting for a debtor country to default on its obligations. It is advised that it put aside any such temptation. The country doing so will likely eliminate any prospect for obtaining credit in the future. Developing countries do need financing for the capital goods produced in industrial countries, which embody new technology, and for other imports if they are to develop. Credit lines likely would not be forthcoming to a defaulting country.

Circumstances that brought both developed and developing countries the debt problem are now clear. The huge increase in debt between 1973 and 1978 coincided with the first Organization of Petroleum Exporting Countries (OPEC) oil price increase. The further doubling of oil prices in 1979 added the second debt explosion. The third big increase came during the worldwide recession of 1982–1983. The debt grew from $130 billion in 1973 to $686 billion in 1983 to $1.3 trillion in 1989.

Blame for the creation of the debt problem has been attributed not only to OPEC for raising the price of oil, but to bankers for making uncollectible loans and to high interest rates and sluggish growth in industrial countries. Many countries, nevertheless, managed to come through these disturbances without major debt increases. For instance, Asian countries even managed to improve their economic situations during the 1970s and 1980s. The bulk of the debt explosion occurred in Latin America, Africa, and some European countries. The United States itself has become the world's largest debtor as a result of its cumulative current account deficits of the 1980s. According to some observers, the common characteristics shared by the United States and international debtors such as Latin American countries were the maintenance of overvalued exchange rates for too long and the use of international credit to finance domestic consumption at the expense of investment. The similarity between the United States and other debtor countries is probably overdrawn. Unlike some developing countries, the United States continues to be an attractive country in which to invest.

CHARACTERISTICS OF SUCCESSFUL ADJUSTMENT

Why were some countries more successful than others in dealing with debt-associated problems? Several reasons come readily to mind.[2] These include the role of prices, including interest rates and markets, in the economy; stability in the monetary environment, including prudent management of the stock of money; an outward-oriented growth strategy; and, some would add, realistic exchange controls.

Our theory and experience suggest that prices, including interest rates, should reflect actual market conditions. They do not always do so. In good part, governments use the interest rate and other prices as a tool in their attempts to stimulate economic growth. Such manipulation of prices is not successful, to judge from the record.

In its sixth World Development Report, the World Bank examines the way developing countries control prices, including interest rates, exchange rates, and wages, as well as many others.[3] In one sample of developing countries, the World Bank finds that prices in the 1970s were controlled least in Malawi and most in Ghana, with a wide range in between. The bank used its index of price distortions to estimate what each country's growth was and then compared that estimate with what actually happened. The evidence shows that growth depends on many things (e.g., resources and political stability), apart from price distortion. Nevertheless, price distortion could explain about one-third of the variation in growth among countries. As the bank succinctly puts it, "Prices do matter for growth."

The more farsighted governments should and do take such evidence seriously. They understand that entrepreneurial skill and human capital, rather than politicians and bureaucrats, are the mainsprings of development. Moreover, it is extremely difficult to dismantle official controls over the direction of credit and investment once they are established.

Even so, no developed country has found that merely establishing the appropriate financial framework—proper supervision, prudent lending, the absence of fraud—is the end of its task. For instance, until recently governments would allow foreign banks to establish themselves within domestic banking systems and give them free rein there. Few local banks, it was argued, would be able to compete. Every country feels the need for a home-grown financial sector because of the central role banks play in economic and monetary policy.

Most developing countries share another characteristic. They all fail to cast the commercial banking net wide enough. Artisans and farmers, who typically comprise between 50 and 80 percent of the total labor force, rely on family, friends, or money lenders for credit. Lending institutions such as the government typically favor larger economic units. Subsidized credit, moreover, means rationing the amount available, usually at the expense of smaller operators.

Developing countries also share a lack of confidence in financial institutions, which results in weak banks and weakening confidence in paper assets, generally making it difficult for a long-term capital market to develop. Gold holdings in many of these countries underscore the lack of confidence in financial institutions. Several of these countries need to widen their financial markets to get more people to hold bank money. They also need to deepen their capital markets so that institutions can give better service to individual companies' financial needs.

Failure to allow the market to play its role almost assures that money and the monetary system will not be allowed to play a nondiscriminatory and autonomous role within the constraints of a rules-based policy system so necessary to ensure the preservation of economic and monetary stability in the country. It assures that money will slip into the political arena and become a political issue. Its manipulation to pursue changing goals and objectives will make money capricious, subject to varying political objectives, and incompatible with a stable monetary order. Monetary manipulation then assures the instability and inflation so characteristic of many emerging and debtor countries.

There are important external constraints to national sovereignty that place limits on money and monetary policy in these nations. In effect, the evidence suggest that the money supply in these countries grows at a rate that over the long run maintains equilibrium in the foreign balance. Monetary authorities cannot influence excess money stock unless they are also willing to change the exchange rate.

All of this, of course, is consistent with the monetarist or quantity theory of money position on the importance of structuring the monetary system so it will not fall prey to manipulation for political purposes. It underscores that money and the monetary system must be allowed to play a nondiscriminatory, autonomous role within the constraints of a rules-based policy system. At the same time, such a policy system of rules will serve to constrain the bureaucracy, the elite, and other interests from the use of monetary manipulation to serve their immediate interests.

The money printing and manipulating monopoly of a nation-state is the heart of the bureaucratic system. Given the records of many emerging countries and others, a printing press can be very dangerous. These countries can either use some stable currency or constrain their bureaucracies within a rules-based system.

IMPORTANCE OF EXPORT-ORIENTED STRATEGY

The importance of an export-oriented growth strategy is underscored. Countries experiencing the greatest debt problems focused their growth strategy on import substitution as against export promotion. Essentially such a strategy attempts to develop domestic industries that produce goods to displace imports—thus reducing dependence on imports and exposure to foreign shocks. The strategy promotes so-called infant industries in the form of tariffs, quotas, and subsidies. Even when well managed, such industries are inefficient. They cannot compete on the international market. Since their market size is limited to the domestic market, they usually cannot enjoy economies of scale available to firms participating in the larger international market.

The strategy of import substitution violates a basic premise put forth by Adam Smith in his classic *Wealth of Nations*. It is better, advised Smith, to promote exports, because success in foreign markets requires efficient production, favorable relative prices, and competent managers capable of carrying out the tasks at hand. There is also a tendency for a country adapting an export strategy to opt for an undervalued currency. As a consequence, its import demands will tend to be more modest than otherwise, so the country will be able to finance such imports from the proceeds of the exports without acquiring a large foreign debt. If the country does not resort to foreign borrowing, it may do so in relative comfort because of its export expansion, which will hold its debt-export ratio to reasonable levels. It will also enjoy large gains in labor productivity because of the economies of scale provided by a larger foreign market. In effect, Asian countries such as Japan, South Korea, and Taiwan are recent examples of Adam Smith's argument that the division of labor is limited only by the size of the market.

Of course, a country is not likely to succeed in carrying out an export-oriented strategy if its currency is overvalued with respect to the rest of the world's currencies. An overvalued currency makes it difficult for a country to export; it encourages imports, and current account deficits are the likely result. These deficits are then typically financed by borrowing abroad. Many Latin American countries whose currencies were overvalued as judged by purchasing power/parity criteria during the 1970s and early 1980s are a case in point.

There are positive aspects to an overvalued currency. In the very short run, domestic consumers enjoy goods and services, including travel abroad, that are inexpensive in terms of domestic currency. Some observers would place the United States in such a category for the period 1980–1985, when high U.S. interest rates attracted foreign capital, which enabled the country to finance a current account deficit.

Not all countries had such an option. Latin American countries, as well as others, financed their current account deficits by borrowing from commercial banks. For example, Mexico, an oil producer, was unwilling or unable to take corrective action when oil prices broke and undercut the high value of its currency. It resorted to heavy borrowing abroad and became the second largest Latin American debtor, as its debt rose from $8.6 billion in 1973 to $82 billion in 1982.

Conditions in a number of countries are also further complicated by inappropriate and counterproductive exchange controls. Asian countries, for instance, managed to conserve foreign exchange by holding down nonessential imports. Many Latin American countries, on the other hand, were unable to do so, with the result that their current account deficits grew rapidly. Argentina, Mexico, and Venezuela come readily to mind as examples of countries where massive capital flights occurred, further increasing their debt problems.

A CATALOG OF SOLUTIONS

All sorts of proposals for the solution of the debt problem are put forth. Creditor countries are urged to make economic adjustments so as to facilitate adjustment in debtor countries. According to the International Monetary Fund, some developing debtor countries burdened with debt and faced with calls from creditors for economic reforms expect to gain "limited short-term domestic benefits" from such reforms and, therefore, lack the necessary incentives to pursue them. The net effect may be to undermine political support for policies that in the longer run would clearly improve welfare in the debtor countries.

Little support is to be found in such organizations as the IMF for debt forgiveness as an alternative to a comprehensive and workable plan to reduce world debt. In the IMF's view, global schemes for general debt forgiveness would not address the specific problems of individual countries. Moreover, such schemes typically carry serious difficulties in design, finance, and moral hazards. Furthermore, it is unlikely that these schemes would provide appropriate incentives for policy adjustments. In the IMF's view, the best approach for debt relief is on a case-by-case basis between official creditors and individual debtor countries. The IMF argues that the private sector could do more to support growth in those countries that are undertaking adjustment programs.

Creditors could also do more to encourage creditors to assist in the readjustment process in debtor countries by allowing for greater flexibility in accounting and banking regulations when renegotiation of loan terms take place. In addition, a more comprehensive framework for negotiation between debtors and creditors could encourage the two sides to work more effectively to realize the growth potential of debtor countries and thus improve their creditworthiness.

A satisfactory solution would require that banks play an important role because of their unique characteristics. For instance, large world banks, unlike some of the smaller banks, have a long-standing relationship with a given country that enables them to take a long-term view when dealing with their foreign clients. They tend to have less incentive to declare a default on loans. Many of these foreign loans are unsecured foreign government loans or are guaranteed by a foreign government. As a result, debt servicing may be interrupted, but most, although not necessarily all, loans are eventually repaid.

Various proposals put forward as possible solutions to the debt problem include massive refunding operations, mandatory transfer of bank claims to a new international organization, and systematic stretching out of existing maturities. Important support would also include a more automatic supply of short-term liquidity by the Bank for International Settlements (BIS) and the IMF and the creation of a market for bank claims with some official support by central banks. A system of partial guarantees by uni- or multilateral world institutions, not national governments, to help commercial banks make new loan commitments and adequate surveillance by the IMF to ensure that new lending will support sound economic policies are also methods that would work toward assisting developing debtor countries.

This does not mean that developing debtor countries will be relieved from dealing with long-run problems related to the structural aspects of the debt crisis—essential problems with great social implications and effects on employment and population, natural resources and energy, innovation, and capital formation. Similar structural problems are faced in the recovery of the developed creditor countries as well. If developed creditor nations are able to maintain monetary stability and avoid inflation, forgoing protectionist measures and keeping the debt issue in the proper perspective as an opportunity to promote global cooperation, the world will be better for it.

Market-oriented debt reduction approaches in the 1980s attracted considerable attention of both creditor and debtor countries. The growing popularity of such approaches is the recognition that debtor countries are unlikely to repay in full on their contractual obligations. The evidence abounds in the growing secondary market, where obligations of many debtor countries are traded in large and varying discounts.

The rapid deals present in the secondary debt market can be attributed to two factors. First, during the 1980s, many regional commercial banks for which the Latin American debt is only a small fraction of their assets or capital made sufficient loss provisions and were willing to cut their losses and get out. Second, many debtor countries have made it easier for banks to move out by offering schemes that allow them to capture some of the discount. These approaches or techniques are now called "market-oriented" because they rely to some extent on the market value of debt.

One widely used technique is that of debt-for-equity swaps. The basic idea is that a prospective foreign investor buys a country's debt at the market discount from the original creditor. The purchaser then exchanges the foreign debt at the central bank for local currency either at its face value or, more likely, at a discount somewhere between the face value and the discounted price. The local currency is then used to finance local equity participation. In effect, the operation gives the foreigner a preferential exchange rate. For its part, the debtor country reduces its external debt by the full value, forgoes future interest payments, and may also appropriate part of the discount. Critics of debt-for-equity swaps argue that efforts simply serve to grant a subsidy to foreign investors who could, presumably, have sought equity participation within foreign currency in any event. They also point to the danger of excessive money creation in countries already infected with high inflation. To these perceived shortcomings of debt-for-equity swaps may be added the nationalist concern that such measures simply serve to turn the country's economy over to foreigners.

A more direct means for carrying debt-for-equity swaps is a simple straight buy-back by debtors, assuming that they have access to foreign exchange. For example, private firms in Mexico have reduced their foreign debt by more than half by offering to buy back their debt at a discount with appropriate foreign exchange funds. These matters are relatively simple to carry out in the private sector because of the limited number of creditors and debtors involved, so that agreements on the discount rate are more readily reached. Much more complicated are the buy-backs of sovereign debt incurred by bank syndicates. A major difficulty with such an approach is to get all syndicated creditors to agree to changes in the terms of loans in order to allow the buy-back. A modified version of debt buy-backs is for the debtor to swap old debts at a discount with its creditors for long term fixed-rate (or exit) bonds. A major advantage of this approach is that since it is not a cash operation, agreement from all creditors is not necessary under the standard conditions of syndicated loans.

Another method is the so-called debt-for-trade swaps between indebted countries. In this method, about 40 percent of the trade of developing countries takes place among themselves, thereby providing an opportunity to use debt-for-trade swaps. Still another method advanced by academicians is debt-for-development, whereby a portion of the country's debt could be used to promote university research and development as well as investment in the human agent, which in many debtor countries is all too often a major obstacle to development.

Yet another option for creditors to choose in negotiating with debtors would link former U.S. Secretaries of the Treasury Baker's and Brady's plans. This proposal, advanced by a prominent French banker and an Argentine financial expert, would create a guarantee fund that would ensure future delivery of debtor country exports.[4] Accordingly, the $20 billion made available by the IMF and the World Bank in response to the debt relief plan put forward in March 1989 by then Secretary Brady would be used to guarantee contracts for delivery worth up to $20 billion of debtor country commodities. The delivery guarantees would presumably enable debtor countries to enter into long-term contracts to sell part of their future commodity exports. These contracts would then serve as collateral to borrow fresh money from banks. The money would be used to buy back the debt at a discount.

Estimates made by investment bankers suggest that by entering a 10-year contract for 20 percent of its annual exports, Venezuela could obtain approximately 13 billion—an amount that would have significantly reduced its $24 billion debt outstanding in 1989. A similar estimate for Brazil would give it $18.5 billion with which to reduce its then (1989) $61 billion commercial debt.

The private French banker's proposal emphasizes that the official funds used as a delivery guarantee pool could make available money to be used for debt reduction that far exceeded the $20 billion that international institutions in 1989 were willing to lend for that purpose. Moreover, under the plan in place in 1989, the $20 billion to finance debt relief wold first be added onto the debt burden of borrowing countries. The proposed plan provides that money borrowed against future exports would be self-liquidating upon delivery of the goods. Furthermore, the proposal does not represent a mortgage of the national heritage. This has already occurred the moment the government signed the initial contracts. The plan of profiting from the discount on the debt purchased enhances the value of exports that normally would have been used to prepay the full value of the debt. Export credit agencies in the industrial countries agreed to participate in financing future material imports at a level much more than the $20 billion in official funds that could become available.

The most likely exports from debtor countries that would be financed under such a scheme are commodities for which a large international market exists, in fairly standardized variety and at prices that are quoted regularly on at least one organized exchange—in such commodities as oil, iron ore, sugar, cocoa, cotton, coffee, cars, and meat and fish products. The actual price paid would be the price at the time of delivery. Revenue shortfalls occur if the delivery price used to value the contract could be made up by either higher delivery accounts or an extended delivery period.

The incentives for importers to set up such long-term supply agreements are provided if the settlement price is an agreed-upon discount from the spot price. Commercial banks could have an incentive in lending new money, since the loans would be collateralized by the guarantee fund. The risk assumed by the banks discounting the sales agreements would be not that of the exporter but that of the purchaser, or of the guarantor in case of undelivery, according to proponents of the plan. To ensure that the export proceeds are used to retire existing debt, the payments could be made to a trustee under irrevocable instructions to disburse the money only for repurchasing debt. Since the products would have to be exported, delivery defaults would be rare, and it would be easy and inexpensive to extend such guarantees.

IN RETROSPECT

The principle of debt reduction in the Brady plan has much to recommend it, even though debt relief does have its problems. Bad loans, however, are the fault of both borrower and lender. When countries that should be experiencing an inflow of capital to finance development are instead exporting it, the situation is indeed critical.

The banks are in no hurry to be forthcoming to their debtors. They are receiving interest. They have managed, for the most part, to build up substantial reserves against potential losses. They say their obligations require a hard line. A bank is not a philanthropy even where their might be compelling reasons for generosity. It must try to conserve assets. Nonetheless, there is the suspicion that banks see some of the debtor countries as of strategic importance to the United States and thus a bargaining point to influence the U.S. government to step in and bail them out of their mistakes with such guarantees as the World Bank or others may provide.

The Brady proposal is an important departure from most of the 1980s, which emphasized continued new lending by the banks and international financial institutions. The key to the Brady plan, announced in March 1989, was the introduction of official collateral from the IMF, the World Bank, the Inter-American Development Bank, and the Japanese government in exchange for a reduction in bank claims. In essence, the restoration of confidence is the central element in the Brady plan. The resumption of private capital inflows and repatriation of capital resulting from this confidence has made the plan financially workable in terms of balance of payment flows. The fact that the plan is market-oriented and quasi-voluntary significantly assisted countries in gaining market access. On balance, the Brady plan was a success.[5]

NOTES

1. William Cline, "Managing International Debt: How One Big Battle Was Won," *The Economist*, February 18, 1995, Vol. 334, No. 7902, pp. 17–19. See also George Macesich, *World Debt and Stability* (New York: Praeger, 1991); H. W. Singer and S. Sharma (eds.), *Economic Development and World Debt* (London: The Macmillan Press, Ltd., 1989).

2. See George Macesich, *World Banking and Finance: Cooperation versus Conflict* (New York: Praeger, 1984).

3. World Bank, *Development Report* (Washington: World Bank, 1983).

4. Carl Gewirtz, "Gambit for Third World Debt Burden: Baker's Plan Linked to Experts," *International Herald Tribune* (June 21, 1989), pp. 11 and 15.

5. William Cline, "Managing International Debt: How One Big Battle Was Won," *The Economist*, February 18, 1995, Vol. 334, No. 7902, p. 18.

8

A Common Market Culture:
The Role of Ideas

PROMOTING A COMMON MARKET CULTURE

The ongoing transformation of the various national economies of the world and their integration is one of the most important events of the post-cold war world. Borders have opened and surges of capital, ideas, and people have promoted a common market culture. Mutual fund companies and big corporations have poured capital into the various emerging markets of the world at an unprecedented pace since the fall of the Berlin Wall in 1989.

Much of the transformation processes in the various economies can be attributed to what really amounts to a new world leadership group created since the 1950s. Beginning in the 1950s, many young people from abroad flocked to American universities to earn advanced degrees, particularly in economics and finance. Many returned home to advocate and push for reform and free market policies. In many respects, they form a network of intellectuals and policy makers who exchange information and advice. Many have since become leaders in their respective countries. They share English as a common language, personal communications, as well as a cosmopolitan democratic and free market outlook for the most part.

TIME LAGS

Economists, and others, agree on the importance of ideas and the considerable lag between these ideas and their execution. John Maynard Keynes put the issue succinctly at the end of his *General Theory*: "Practical men, who believe themselves to be quite exempt from any intellectual influences, are usually slaves of some defunct economist. Most men in authority, who hear voices in the air, are distilling their frenzy from some academic scribbler of a few years back."[1]

There are reasons for the existence of the lag. Milton Friedman argues that one reason why economists have a difficult time convincing policy makers is that they assume policy makers always wish to do the right thing.[2] That is, they assume that policy makers have the public interest as their primary concern. Policy makers primarily think of their own interest, although they believe that it coincides with the public interest. Not every politician and/or bureaucrat in the emerging market economies welcomes the political transformation accompanied by a massive shift toward economic liberalization. In particular, the curtailment of government regulation, privatization of state industries, and favoring of foreign investment reduces, if not eliminates, a hitherto profitable venture for many of these policy makers and their cultivated taste for discretionary authority. This is certainly consistent with Friedman's view.

It is thus that Friedman notes that it may do little good to talk directly to policy makers. Instead of direct talk he suggests three options. The first option is that economists can continue to talk to the public in general, arguing, for instance, the wisdom of free trade instead of protectionism. This will take time, but its chances for success are probably greater than trying to convince an individual legislator, who can identify at the polls how he or she would gain by supporting an individual piece of protectionist legislation. For economists to attack each piece of protectionist legislation separately is likely to be a useless exercise. It is better if they do not dissipate their energies and aim rather at educating the public in general about tariffs and the virtues of free trade.

The second method is to get the public to press for institutional changes, such as a constitutional amendment barring any and all trade restrictions. This procedure, according to Friedman, has two advantages. First, the burden to the consumer of foreign trade restraints is considerable enough that it merits his or her being informed about it—provided the information could be put to effective use. Second, a constitutional amendment requires a single crusade because once enacted it has a continuing effect, whereas a series of crusades or efforts are required to defeat individual tariff proposals.

ROLE OF CRISIS

The third way is to keep all options open for times of crisis. It is in crises that major restructural changes are likely to occur. The American federal deficit, for instance, is forcing people to think seriously about how to control federal spending. On this score at least, the practical effect of the deficit is good.

The crises of the late 1960s and 1970s, including the oil and debt crisis, opened the way for floating exchange rates. Friedman and others had argued for years about the advantages of floating exchange rates compared with a system of fixed and administered exchange rates. A situation calling for drastic action had not occurred until the gold drain from the United States in the 1960s.

It is unlikely that floating exchange rates would have been adopted had they not been discussed and accepted by the majority of economists. Floating rates thus provided an option available to society. Had they not been available as an option, undoubtedly something else would have been put in place, and probably without the benefit of the thorough-going discussion to which flexible exchange rates were subject.

Keynesian ideas also benefited from the interwar crisis (between World War I and World War II). These ideas became all the more receptive as a viable option due especially to the crises and depression years of the 1930s. Other episodes in history provide illustrations of crisis-propelled reforms. For instance, the establishment and demise of the Second Bank of the United States (1816–1836) followed the War of 1812, and the passage of the National Bank Act of 1863 occurred during the tragic years of the American Civil War. The founding of the Federal Reserve System in 1913 and its reorganization in the 1930s are illustrations, as are the recent fall of the Berlin Wall and the end of the cold war, which accelerated worldwide reform.

It is a mistake, as Keynes pointed out, to dispute the potency of ideas, both when they are right and when they are wrong. Ideas are more powerful than is commonly thought. The world is ruled by little else. It takes time, however, for ideas to be executed. Friedman notes that it was 70 years before the doctrines of Adam Smith's *Wealth of Nations* were adopted as public policy in Great Britain.[3] Keynes comments that in the field of economic and political philosophy there are not many people who are influenced by new theories after they are 25 or 30 years of age, so the ideas applied by most bureaucrats and politicians are not likely to be the newest. He concludes his *General Theory* with a sentence that aptly summarizes the point at issue: "But sooner or later, it is ideas, not vested interests, which are dangerous for good or evil."[4]

DIFFUSION OF IDEAS

Some ideas are more readily received than others. Milton Friedman, for instance, developed the idea of a broad-based low-rate tax system. More than 25 years later, Senators Bob Packwood and Bill Bradley pushed for the adoption of such a tax system in the American Congress. On the other hand, Friedman's ideas on monetary growth rates, which he elaborated from those of earlier scholars, have not received the acceptance they merit.

The lack of receptiveness is particularly evident in the central banking community. This can be attributed in good part to cultivated taste for discretionary policy on the part of the community. It can also be attributed to the lack of an appropriate agent that can serve to move these ideas from the theoretical discussion of economists into practical application by central bankers and monetary authorities. It is thus useful to consider the problem of receptiveness to gain some insight on how ideas are diffused within the organization of government, including central banks. For this purpose and, in particular, for the role of crises, it is useful to turn to medicine and its branches of epidemiology and clinical toxicology for analytical techniques to explain the spread of economic ideas.[5] Epidemiology studies the spread of diseases, specifying a cause-effect relationship between the disease and the victim. Toxicology studies the impact of toxins on the human victims. Social organizations have much in common with the human organism.

Since bureaucracies, including central banks, are social organisms composed of individuals, there really is nothing novel in the application of medical and/or biological categories and concepts to economic issues. In fact, Alfred Marshall urged economists to look to biology for useful insights into economic problems. In his view, biological concepts are preferable to mechanical, since economics is, after all, a life science. Even earlier Francois Quesnay, a physician, applied his medical knowledge in discovering and applying the circular flow mechanism to economic phenomena.

The spread of ideas is similar to the spread of the germ of an epidemic. The germ is spread because carriers carry the infection from its origins through a mechanism to the victim. The methods and processes of how the disease is spread from the source to the possible victim are the special concern of epidemiologists. In their view, the relationship is not simply between the germ and the victim. There is an environment within which a struggle between agent and susceptible host takes place; and in this struggle a disturbing crisis plays an important role to disrupt the balance between the two, thereby enabling the disease to spread.

The actions of toxins in the human body is similar to the spread of ideas within an organization. The toxicologist is primarily concerned with the victim and a toxic agent. He or she studies the relationship in terms of a number of categories.[6] The spread of toxic bacteria, or the idea, is a twofold process. There is the process in the spread of a germ or idea that is first part of the environment. There is the second process of the impact of the germ or idea, which must take place within a specific context. In other words, ideas, like germs, are impersonal, and so have a momentum of their own. It is, however, the individual economist or group of economists who actually put the idea into practice.[7] To do so, they must be part of the bureaucratic apparatus.

In biology, organisms composed of cells are activated by enzyme reaction. Similarly, in social organizations such as a bureaucracy, the cells are the bureaucrats and the enzymes their ideas and attitudes. A bacteria or germ that enters a body inhibits the enzymes within the cell from doing normal work. This may result in a local irritation or enter the bloodstream and nervous system and thus affect the whole body. Toxic substances do not always have a free hand, and their success depends on the functioning of recovery defense mechanisms.

In like manner, new ideas must impact on old and established ways of thinking. As with toxic agents, ideas must affect the enzymes, destroy existing defenses, and transmit the disease to the entire body. They must win over individuals and get accepted at various levels to influence social policy. Bureaucracies, however, have formidable defense systems against "infections" of new ideas and modes of thinking. These include the nature of bureaucratic work—shunning intellectual curiosity and cultivating precedents and previously established and held opinions.

The strength of these defenses depends on the state of the economy and the urgency of the economic problem that needs to be addressed. In other words, a crisis that must be dealt with will weaken or overwhelm the established defenses and thus make possible the acceptance of new ideas.

Ideas do not always have an impact, even though conditions for their acceptance seem favorable. Similarly, the toxicologist has difficulty explaining why a very poisonous substance appears to act selectively on a particular organ or group of organs, whereas the enzyme systems it may be supposed to influence are much more widely distributed. On this score, toxicologists are in no better position than economists to explain unequivocally the tie between economic ideas and policy.

Nevertheless, the analytical approach set out by toxicologists does provide useful insights into the relationship between economic ideas and policy. The social organism has many points in common with the human organism. As a social organism, bureaucracy is composed of many individuals, and the impact of ideas on these individuals and their final outcome are dependent on the process of diffusion, the individuals' resistance, and their positions in their hierarchy. For an idea to be successful, it must have not only many converts, but they must be well-located and powerful. It is the same with a toxin. To do the most damage, the toxin must attack not only with virulence but must also affect the nervous and circulatory systems.

Ambirajan applies the foregoing model to the formulation of monetary policy in India in the 20-year period of 1873–1893.[8] This is a period of considerable monetary uncertainty, not only in India but in many other countries as well. It is also a period in which the course of monetary events perplexed policy makers. The immediate cause of the crisis was a sudden increase in world production of silver and its fall in price. Since India was on the silver standard, the rate of exchange of the Indian rupee also dropped. Decline in the exchange rate was also reinforced by the demonetization of silver by Germany, Denmark, Sweden, Norway, and Holland and the restriction of silver coinage by the Latin Union, comprising France, Belgium, Italy, and Switzerland.[9] India's inability to absorb the surplus of silver was thus the main economic problem that confronted the Indian government.

One consequence of the depreciation of silver was to complicate trade between India and England. Many English economists argued that the solution for the problems of Anglo-Indian trade was a common standard. Orthodox British opinion supported the gold standard. Indian opinion, on the other hand, argued for a bimetallic standard of gold and silver. This was a policy option supported by many continental economists. By 1886, the government of India declared itself as bimetallist. Nevertheless, a bimetallic policy was not adopted by India.

What insights does this episode of Indian monetary have for the relationship between economic ideas and economic policy? In terms of our epidemiological and toxicological model and its categories, we have, according to Ambirajan, first the diffusion of the idea of bimetallism: the *origin*—England and Europe; the *carriers*—British educated civilians; the *mechanism of transmission*—physical contact during leave periods abroad, journals and various other published sources; and the *susceptible host*—Indian bureaucracy. Second is the impact of the idea on policy: the *incubation period*, 1873–1886, the years when the Indian civil servants were becoming converted to bimetallic ideas; the *infection period*, 1886–1892, when the Indian government accepted bimetallist ideas; the *pathogenesis*, when reports and studies at various official levels favored bimetallic standards; the *manifestation of illness*, characterized by (1) recommendation of bimetallic policy by Indian authorities to British home office, (2) proposals to introduce monetary reforms in India as a first step toward adoption of a bimetallic policy, and (3) suggestions welcoming international bimetallism; and the *state of health*, which was serious due to foreign exchange burden and problems in increasing domestic tax resources.

The idea of bimetallism, according to Ambirajan, "spread to such an extent that it demolished the entire system of defense mechanism as far as the organization of bureaucracy in India was concerned. However, the one major problem was that the ultimate authority for policy formation was vested in the British Cabinet."[10] In the case of monetary policy in India, the fiscal decision rested with the British cabinet when economic policies affected British interests. Thus it was necessary not only for a new idea "to destroy the defense mechanisms in the Indian side of the bureaucracy but also on the British side of decision making [sure] . . . all the mechanisms of defense against new ideas in the British decision making apparatus were strong and effective."[11]

It was always difficult to give a precise answer to the influence of monetary ideas in monetary policy at any particular point in time. The variables are many, and their span is usually a generation or more. On the other hand, precision is really not necessary. What is important is that we gain insight into the processes by which ideas affect policies. For this purpose, Ambirajan's discussion of Indian monetary experience, by drawing on epidemiological and toxicological categories, provides a useful model for other monetary experiences. So too is his conclusion that individual economists or groups of economists actually enable an idea to be put into practice. Such economists, however, must be part of the administrative apparatus of a country.

For instance, the lack of receptivity for Friedman's idea for a monetary rule may be due to the lack of properly positioned economists sympathetic to a monetary rule in the country's administrative system for monetary and banking affairs. The idea for a monetary rule itself has a long history, dating to the 19th century. George S. Tavalas, for instance, has traced the growth rule back to the writings of Jeremy Bentham and Henry Thornton, as well as to the neglected writings of John Gray during the 1830s and 1840s.[12]

Antipathy to the ideas of the "Chicago School" are thus an inadequate reason. For it was Jeremy Bentham writing at the beginning of the 19th century, who used the quantity theory of money framework to argue that short-term changes in money influence both prices and output. He argued over the longer term, that a country's wealth grows independently of changes in the money supply. In the long run, money affects only the price level. Bentham thought that price level stabilization was a necessary goal that could be achieved by increases in monetary circulation that kept pace with increases in wealth. These views are shared by Friedman and contemporary monetarists (modern quantity theorists).

Henry Thornton also shared Bentham's concern with methods for achieving price stability, and like Bentham he was a quantity theorist. Price level stability could be achieved, according to Thornton, by limiting increases in the quantity of money to the "natural progress of commerce" and by allowing it to "vibrate only within certain limits."[13]

Although Bentham and Thornton provide us with early examples for a monetary rule, it is the English economist John Gray (1799–1883) and his contribution that is perhaps even more directly related to Friedman's rule.[14] He argued as early as 1848 that for stability to be achieved in a money market economy, it is necessary that the money supply, which he defined as consisting of gold coin and bank notes backed by securities, should increase just as fast as the economy's total marketable commodities but no faster. It is instability in the money supply that provides peril for the economy, according to Gray. If the money supply does not grow as fast as the aggregate supply of goods is increased, prices and profits fall and a reduction in output follows. For prices to remain stable and thus provide a framework favorable for economic growth, a monetary growth rule should be put in place. Contemporary monetarists led by Milton Friedman advocate such a rule and for almost exactly the same reasons as did Gray.

Many of Gray's contributions, including the monetary growth rule, gathered dust for almost 100 years before being resurrected in the 1920s and 1930s by American economists William T. Foster and Waddill Catchings, and then through the monetary writings of Paul Douglas at the University of Chicago.[15] They too argued that depressions were caused by the failure of the supply of money and credit to keep pace with the long-term growth in economic output. The consequence of such a failure would be a fall in the general price level and ultimately a decline in profits and output, as Gray and Foster argued earlier. Catchings and Douglas questioned the full employment assumption of classical economists. In essence, Foster, Catchings, and Douglas refined and extended Gray's monetary framework, which is very similar to that in use by contemporary monetarists.

Douglas was also aware of the lags in discretionary changes in the money supply. He argued that stability in the general level of prices and employment can be achieved by allowing the quantity of money to increase at the rate of 3 to 4 percent per year. The monetary growth rule pushed by Douglas in the 1930s is certainly consistent with Friedman's later claim that his monetary economics represents a direct continuation of the Chicago monetary tradition of that period.[16] The Chicago monetary tradition, with its emphasis on a monetary growth rule, is an old and venerable one.

It is this tradition, revived and refurbished in Milton Friedman's "Money and Banking Workshop" at the University of Chicago, that pervades contemporary monetarist thought and practice. It is also because of Friedman's efforts that monetary economics is exciting and concerned with crucial issues. His work changed professional thinking on matters pertaining to the role of money. At the same time, his key role in pushing free markets in place of economic planning as a means for organizing economic activity serves as an inspiration and model for academics, policy makers, businesspeople, and others with responsibility for the on-going transformation processes in the world's emerging markets.[17]

Harry Johnston, for example, has described changes in monetary theory as owing much to Friedman's efforts, which gave monetary analysis "a central place to expectations about future price movements," and to Fisher's distinction between real and money rates of interest—in contrast to Keynesian analysis, which always started with the assumption of stable prices. This theory, empirical research, and monetary economics were steered toward concepts and methods far more appropriate to the inflationary and necessary development of the past decade than Keynesian economics was capable of providing.[18]

More recently, the failure of fine tuning the money supply is being confused with the failure of monetarism and the futility of monetarist policy prescriptions, including adoption of a monetary growth rule.[19] For the most part, this view can be attributed to the failure on the part of Keynesians newly converted to monetary fine-tuning to read and understand correctly the historic record between changes in the money supply and in such major economic magnitudes as income, interest rates, price levels, exchange rates, output, and employment. We simply do not have the type of knowledge necessary to make fine-tuning of monetary policy successful. Such evidence as we do have argues strongly against fine-tuning; thus the swings between slow and rapid monetary growth in 1980, 1981, and 1982. These efforts, according to Friedman, "destabilized the money market and lengthened and deepened the 1981–82 recession."[20] In sum, "money is too important to be left to central bankers."[21]

In terms of epidemiological and toxicological categories, thus far this idea for a monetary growth rule has not been able to destroy the defense mechanisms of central bank bureaucracy or convince all economists of its appropriateness, as our discussion indicates. The defense mechanism against new (old) ideas in the central bank decision-making apparatus continues strong and effective. The carriers of the money growth idea are, for the time being, improperly positioned or lacking the bureaucratic apparatus to carry it out.

This idea, as in the example of the germ, is part of the environment and has been so for almost 200 years. It is not yet a part of the bureaucratic apparatus of central banks. A future crisis will likely disrupt the balance in the environment between the agent and susceptible host, enabling the idea of a monetary growth rule to spread within central banks, as in our epidemiological illustration.

As in the Indian experience, however, it may not be sufficient to convert only the central bank bureaucracy in the United States. It may be necessary for the American presidential office to accept the idea of a monetary growth rule as well, if we are to take seriously the results of recent studies indicating the importance of presidential influence on the Federal Reserve System's operations. It is only then that we can expect to observe a change in the cultivated tastes for discretionary monetary policy on the part of the monetary authority. As in our epidemiological illustration, the process may be accelerated by the occurrence of a crisis that may so change the environment as to make monetary authorities and the financial community susceptible to different ideas.

Another example of an idea that has, thus far, not been able to destroy the formidable bureaucratic-nationalistic defense mechanism in place in many of the former socialist countries of East Europe is that of market democracy as an organizing principle for reform. The rhetoric of market democracy, individual rights, rule of law, and related issues is profuse in many of these countries. The practice, however, falls far short.

In fact, taking its cue from many of the ideas presented by Milton Friedman and the tradition of the University of Chicago, the Center for Yugoslav-American Studies, Research, and Exchange at Florida State University and its programs in comparative policy studies served to promote the many lessons of successful reform in Eastern Europe and particularly in Yugoslavia in the period 1961–1991. The Center's joint academic programs promoted an open dialogue on the idea of market democracy as the culmination of more than 300 years of economics. This idea is centered on a theory of pluralistic democracy in a free market-oriented society with private property and civil rights transcending narrow nationalism, wherein everyone has the freedom to develop. It does not share the Marxist pretension that commandeering society is the one way to assure prosperity and freedom. It is equally skeptical of nationalism, which has replaced Marxism in many of these countries as the guiding spirit of government.[22]

An organizing idea or principle for reform is important. It serves as a guide for people to think about a political economy. Without such a principle, the state will again become dominant. The political and economic structure will be taken over by well-organized special interests to the detriment of the rest of society. Reform will simply serve to perpetuate the interests of the ever-active political elite and bureaucracy.

There are many lessons of successful reform. At least two, however, should be underscored. One is that all the elements of a well-designed reform program are interdependent, mutually supporting, and interactive. It is folly to focus on one or another of the elements in the program to the exclusion of the rest. Another lesson is that speed is essential. The total program may take years to carry through before the benefits become visible. The costs, however, appear immediately. Move too slowly and the consensus that supports the reform can collapse. It is uncertainty, not speed, that endangers a reform program and casts doubt on the government's credibility to carry it out.

The idea of nationalism can be an important force in reform and national renewal. Unfortunately, its negative side is likely to subvert reform and market democracy. In particular, the kind of nationalism arising in Eastern and Central Europe, with undertones of jealousy, rivalry, and exclusion, will not support the compromise and tolerance that market democracy requires. The tragedy of Yugoslavia and its successor states since 1991 demonstrates the futility of promoting narrow nationalism.

The former ruling Marxist ideology clearly failed to encourage people in this area of Europe to work their way through the gradual accommodation that brought other Europeans to realize that they must live harmoniously together. Strengthening a sense of nationalism thus becomes another catch-up job for these countries, along with all the other serious problems before them. It will, if anything, make solutions to all their other problems even more difficult.

An example of a more successful diffusion of free market reformist ideas is Latin America. Many of the region's best and brightest are an elite of economists and intellectuals who were trained in such leading American universities as the University of Chicago, Harvard, MIT, and Yale and went home to promote free market ideas from the vantage point of real political power. In their maturity and influence, they have emerged together as a network of academics and policy makers that reaches from campus to conference to consultancy. The success of reform owes much to their influence.

One observer notes that the typical cabinet minister in Latin America in the 1990s is a person in his mid-forties with a U.S. Ph.D. earned in the late 1970s who has spent his life in the academy or a think tank and then, after the debt crisis of the 1980s, became minister of finance or another major portfolio. In fact, the first Latin American country to build an academic bridge to the United States was Chile. The country has become the intellectual hothouse for the region's economic revolution. For this Chile owes much to the University of Chicago and to the ideas of Milton Friedman, Arnold Harbarger, D. Gale Johnson, T. W. Schultz, and others in the Department of Economics. A cohort of Chicago-trained Chilean economists, known for free market ideas and a willing patron to implement them, is known as the "Chicago Boys."

General Augusto Pinochet, who assumed power from socialist President Salvador Allende in a 1973 coup, had little in the way of an economic program. At the urging of Chile's business community, he turned to the Chicago Boys. Thereafter the Chicago Boys pushed forward a reform program for Chile that managed eventually to turn the country around and on course to prosperity. There were painful lessons in the 1970s and some backsliding on the part of Pinochet. By the 1980s, however, the Chilean model, which includes careful controls on speculative foreign capital and strong incentives for investment, is the one that country after country in Latin America has emulated.

No transformation taking place in a cultural environment long accustomed to broad swings of the political pendulum and abrupt reversals of fortune can be called permanent. It is possible that sometime in the future another set of ideas may come to dominate the region. There are hopes that the shrinkage of government, the demystification of the state, and the democratic impulse will doom official corruption, a fixture of Latin American political life for decades.

Certainly, the rapid collapse of the Soviet empire suggests that ideas are seldom firmly entrenched. They do need the strong support of the best and brightest and carriers of ideas willing and properly positioned in the bureaucratic apparatus to carry them out. A slow inner death had transformed the Communist Party and system into an empty shell of rotten cynicism that crumbled when it met serious resistance from democratic ideals. Even the carriers themselves ceased to believe in the communist system and no longer pushed for its preservation.[23] Quite simply, the communists, or ar least the most intelligent party leaders, had no belief in the ideals they were supposed to stand for. In fact, as one observer puts it, what distinguished the Gorbachevites in the former Soviet Union was their recognition of imperial defeat and the need to engineer a dignified and peaceful decolonization, if only to save their own skins.[24]

NOTES

1. John Maynard Keynes, *The General Theory of Employment, Interest, and Money* (New York: Harcourt, Brace and World, First Harbinger Edition, 1964), p. 383.

2. Milton Friedman, "Economists and Economic Policy," *Economic Inquiry,* 24 (January, 1986), 1–10.

3. Ibid., p. 1.

4. Keynes, *General Theory,* p. 384.

5. See, for instance, S. Ambirajan, "Economics and Economists in the Formation of a Monetary Policy for India, 1973–1893," *History of Political Economy,* Vol. 9, No. 1 (Spring 1977), pp. 122–143. See also George Macesich, *Monetary Reform and Cooperation Theory* (New York: Praeger, 1989), pp. 57–64.

6. See S. Ambirajan, "Economics and Economists," p. 138, for a discussion of the categories.

7. Ibid., p. 139.

8. Ibid., p. 141.

9. For a discussion of American experience with silver, see Milton Friedman and Anna J. Schwartz, *Monetary History of the United States, 1867–1960* (Princeton, NJ: Princeton University Press for the National Bureau of Research, 1963), Chapter 3.

10. Ambirajan, "Economics and Economists," p. 142.

11. Ibid., p.142.

12. George S. Tavalas, "Some Initial Formulations of the Monetary Growth Rate Rule," *History of Political Economy,* Vol. 9, No. 4 (Winter 1977), pp. 535–547.

13. Ibid., p. 541.

14. Ibid.

15. See George S. Tavalas, "Some Further Observations on the Monetary Economics of Chicagoans and Non-Chicagoans," *Southern Economic Journal,* Vol. 42 (April 1976), pp. 685–92.

16. See Milton Friedman, "Comments on the Critics," *Journal of Political Economy,* Vol. 80 (September–October, 1972), pp. 932–41.

17. See the interview with Milton Friedman in Gene Epstein's "Public Enemy No. 1? To a Nobel Laureate, It's Big Government, Not Budget Gaps," *Barron's,* The Dow Jones Business and Financial Weekly, September 4, 1995, p. 41.

18. Harry Johnson, "The Nobel Milton," *The Economist,* Vol. 23 (October 1976), p. 95.

19. For a response to the alleged failure of monetarism, see Milton Friedman, "M1's Hot Streak Gave Keynesians a Bad Idea," *Wall Street Journal* (September 18, 1986), p. 32, and the interview with Milton Friedman in Gene Epstein's article in *Barron's* (September 4, 1995), p. 41.

20. Ibid.

21. Ibid.

22. See George Macesich, *Reform and Market Democracy* (New York: Praeger, 1991).

23. See the interesting discussion in David Pryce-Jones, *The Strange Death of the Soviet Empire* (New York: Henry Holt and Company, 1995).

24. Orlando Figes, "Without a Fight," *The New York Times Book Review,* September 3, 1995, p. 7.

9

Globalizing Employment Opportunities

FARMING OUT TASKS

The globalization of markets also entails risks of unemployment for skilled workers in many of the developed industrial countries. It is already an issue of concern that some American workers have trained their foreign replacements. One large American insurance firm, for instance, brought programmers from India to the home office and began training them to replace American workers.[1]

In fact, the growing tendency of corporations to farm out tasks to developing countries is widening the gap between the well-to-do economically and others in American society by eliminating some categories of high-skill, high-wage jobs that make up the core of the American middle class. It is difficult to fault the temptation of corporations to use less costly foreign labor given that they are desperate to stay competitive in an increasingly global marketplace.

India is a good example of such tendencies. It has inherited a functioning English-language school system from the days of British rule. It has also emphasized mathematical education. One result is that computer scientists trained at Indian universities come relatively cheap. Experienced programmers command salaries of $1,200 to $1,500 a month compared to $4,000 to $10,000 in the United States. The result has been explosive growth in the number of Indians working in computer programs mainly for the American market, to nearly 70,000 in 1995 from several thousand in the early 1980s.

The apparent exodus of white-collar jobs to developing countries has raised concern from many people, including some economists. In particular, economists argue that though many firms are anxious to make use of the American infrastructure (e.g., good roads, ready access to markets, and related advantages), the fact is that the growing part of the world's economy is based on ideas and information and does not always need such physical proximity as the United States and other developed countries provide.

The rapid integration of global markets has impacted negatively on the real wages in the United States for the semiskilled and unskilled worker, particularly in some selected industries. Other observers point out, however, that it is not just lower wages that made foreign sites so attractive to American industry. It is also, for instance, that American engineers can work on a project during the day and then send it electronically for more work in Asia while they sleep. As a result, many projects can be completed much more quickly than would otherwise be the case. One consequence is that American workers, for instance, also benefit through increased demand for their own output. It is also true that foreign companies cannot continue to count on the availability of cheap skilled labor in emerging market countries.

Even those who dismissed the warnings of various politicians that the dismantling of trade barriers and globalization of markets would lead to a flight of jobs now admit that there may be serious problems abroad. A case in point is NAFTA's one-way street, with Mexico's problems cutting into imports from the United States while its exports are soaring. When NAFTA went into effect on January 1, 1994, proponents were predicting that by the end of 1995 the United States would be running a $9 billion trade surplus with Mexico. Some people were arguing that the reduction in barriers would lead to an additional 200,000 jobs related to exports being created in the United States by 1995.

The United States enjoyed a surplus of more than $1 billion in trade with Mexico during the first six months of 1994. But then came Mexico's economic crisis. American exports to Mexico between January and June 1995 dropped almost 12 percent compared to the same period in 1994, while Mexico's exports to the United States soared by 29 percent.

The drop in American exports to Mexico has been most acute in consumer goods, services, and franchise-related items. A boom in Mexico's borde- located assembly plant exports accounts for most of the jump in the country's exports, these include so-called *maquiladoras* (a Mexican company accorded special treatment that allows it to import duty-free anything needed to carry out production, including raw materials, equipment, machinery, and parts). The labor-intensive, low-wage plants assemble components known as intermediate goods—such as automobile parts, clothing pieces, and electronic components from the United States or elsewhere—to make finished goods for re-export. The gain for the American manufacturer is that the Mexican surge in exports is heavily dependent on the use of intermediate goods.

The impact on the American labor market is suggested by U.S. Labor Department figures, which indicate that 35,000 American workers have applied for retraining assistance after losing their jobs because of NAFTA. The assistance was required under a hotly disputed 1993 side accord to NAFTA designed to protect U.S. labor from the effects of plant relocations to Mexico, where workers earn less in a day than their counterparts earn in an hour. Other observers note, however, that by using the predictions of NAFTA proponents that up to 20,000 jobs would be created with every $1 billion increase in U.S. trade with Mexico, nearly 140,000 American jobs have been lost to Mexico since the 1994–1995 devaluation of the Mexican peso.

It is not only the Mexican re-export industries that are reaping a windfall in exports from NAFTA, but other industries as well. For instance, Mexico's two largest steel manufacturers in 1995 were operating at 100 percent of capacity to meet American demand for cheap steel. Earlier the industry was doing very well if it managed to operate at 65 percent capacity. The devaluation of the peso in terms of the American dollar in 1994–1995 had the effect of placing a 50 percent tariff on all goods exported to Mexico. For all practical purposes, the devaluation removed most of the benefits to American trade from the decline in tariffs under NAFTA, which brought prices down for the Mexican consumer and made U.S. goods affordable. Evidence can be found in any Mexico City supermarket, where high-priced U.S. products have been replaced on shelves by more affordable, lower-quality Mexican goods. Indeed, Mexican advertisements now urge Mexicans not to buy imported products because foreign goods can cost Mexico jobs.

In the aggregate, however, NAFTA probably will have little effect on the U.S. labor market or on U.S. wages, because U.S. workers who will lose their jobs would be far less than 1 percent of the labor force. There will likely be significant employment shifts within and between industries, with unskilled workers bearing the disproportionate burden of the labor adjustment costs at a time when income inequality in the United States is widening. As globalization increases, there is a great incentive for U.S. firms to move, if not to Mexico then to other countries with cheap labor. In the case of the Mexican *maquiladoras*, they are attractive to American firms because of lower labor costs, tax breaks, and proximity to the U.S. market.

It may be some time before Mexico will be able to take its place at the leading edge of science, technology, and other academic endeavors. The problems at the country's leading university in Mexico City (National Antonomaous University of Mexico) underscore the issues.[2] The university, with more than 265,000 students, is the biggest in Latin America. It serves as the best option for a university education and so access to technical, scientific, academic, and business careers for working-class youths all over Mexico. The demand for admissions has more than strained the institution's capacity to accommodate all applicants. In fact, for the academic year 1995–1996, the institution received 152,000 applications for the freshman class, about 132,000 of which were rejected. Some 32,000 were admitted automatically from special high schools in Mexico City that are directly affiliated with the university. The net result is to leave tens of thousands of applicants competing for about 8,000 places.

Matters are further complicated by the fact that there are few low-tuition alternatives outside Mexico City. At the same time, Mexican state universities are slashing enrollment, causing rejection rates to soar. All of this has brought protests from students, potential students, and others. In any case, Mexico has a singular constraint on any ambitions it may have on joining the world's leading industrial countries.

In Mexico, as in other emerging market countries, it is important to meet the major challenge of human resources. These countries must create more jobs and increase incentives to foreign investors. If these efforts are not successful in bringing more of their citizens into productive economic activity, the pursuit of political power for good or ill may be their only option. How successful these efforts will be depends on access of emerging market countries to the markets of industrial countries. There are several centers of economic importance, rather than individual countries, that can provide the economic opportunities for emerging market countries.

ACCESS TO CENTERS OF GROWTH

In fact, there are three centers of economic power that are of singular importance to emerging market countries: the European Union, North America, and East Asia. These regional trading blocs total around 90 percent of world trade and include the most prosperous and developed areas of the world.

I have noted the importance of NAFTA and the free trade agreement concluded by the United States, Canada, and Mexico. This is a free trade that includes about 360 million people, a GNP of about $7 trillion, two rich and developed countries (the United States and Canada), and one emerging market country (Mexico). These countries already account for more than $245 billion of foreign trade among themselves, which is larger than the combined U.S.-Canada trade with Europe. In a radical departure from previous policies, Mexico opened up opportunities for foreign investment, particularly from the United States and Canada.

The United States, of course, has a long-standing role in direct investment in both Canada and Mexico that dates back to the 19th century. Investment by the U.S. in ventures such as railroads, minerals, and forest industries are cases in point. In the period between the wo world wars, U.S. investments abroad increased, especially into Canada. The post-World War II period is characterized by increased U.S. investment in Canada and Europe. The U.S. direct foreign investment in Canada and Mexico exceeds Canadian and Mexican direct investment in the United States.

The market potential of NAFTA for its members is certainly important, particularly in the future. The Latin American market and the Central American market may turn out to provide considerable potential. I have noted that Brazil, Venezuela, Argentina, and Chile will likely provide a significant boost to exporters and importers in the region. These countries have embarked on privatizing many of their state-owned industries and on encouraging foreign investment to upgrade their industries.

The other important center of growth is East Asia. The countries of that area have well demonstrated their ability to combine Western science and technology with their own domestic traits to produce an important world center of economic growth. I have noted elsewhere their unique characteristics, including an important role that the state or government play in industry. These countries have all pursued an export-oriented strategy as the shortest route to economic development. Moreover, all of these countries had a surplus in their merchandise accounts with the United States in the early 1990s. In 1991, U.S. direct investment in Pacific Asia amounted to around $37 billion and Pacific Asian investment in the United States amounted to $90 billion. For all practical purposes, Japan is synonymous with Pacific Asia, because Japanese direct investment in the United States in 1991 amounted to about $87 billion compared to U.S. direct investment in Japan of $23 billion. As a matter of fact, Japan ranked second only to the United Kingdom in the value of foreign direct investment in the United States.

If in fact a Pacific Asian trading bloc emerges in the future, it will no doubt become an important player in the world economic scene. The entire Pacific Asian area grew faster in the early 1990s than the United States and Europe. In the same period, the area was running a trade surplus of around $150 billion a year—the world's largest trade surplus. The problem for these countries is that they are finding it increasingly more difficult to use exports as the leading edge for their economies. To grow faster than the rest of the world, these countries have to capture larger and larger world market shares. It is not likely that other countries will tolerate continued penetration of their markets. Certainly it is clear that Europe and the United States will not tolerate such activities on the part of Pacific Asian countries. In the future, these countries may have to pursue policies designed to stimulate domestic demand, including imports. If Europe and the United States decide to take measures that are designed to compel Japan and other Pacific Asian countries to reduce their trade deficits by buying more U.S. and European products, a Pacific Asian trading bloc may be viewed as a means to protect their economic interests.

The other major center of growth is the European Union (EU). All sorts of efforts have been made by the European member countries of the EU to promote a common market. In fact, before the end of the century, the EU plans to build common foreign and defense policies, unify its monetary policies, and even issue a common currency unit, European Currency Unit, or ECU. To these plans may be added the EU's abandonment of natural tariffs and trade quotas and an adoption of common market standards. Borders will be opened to free travel by citizens of member nations, and continentwide citizenship rules will be established. Considering that many of the member states have been traditional enemies whose differences have plunged the world into war more than once in the past 100 years, it is understandable that many observers are skeptical about how successful the project will be, particularly in such areas as a common currency and common monetary policies. As for foreign policy, European failures in the Yugoslav tragedy are notable indeed.

In any case, a strong Western Europe was of mutual interest to the Europeans and Americans in the postwar period as a bulwark against Soviet expansion. The Marshall Plan aid to Europe, which began in 1947, and the creation of the North American Treaty Organization (NATO) in 1949 served to unite European efforts toward recovery and mutual defense. In 1950 Robert Schuman, French minister of foreign affairs, proposed that France and West Germany pool their coal and steel production as one unit. In 1951, Belgium, France, Italy, Luxembourg, the Netherlands, and West Germany signed the Treaty of Paris, which established the European Coal and Steel Community. In 1957 the European Economic Community (EEC) was created by the Treaty of Rome. Over the next few years, the organization was converted from a customs union to an economic union that was designed to allow the free flow of capital and labor from one country to another.

By 1979, a move toward complete integration was made with the creation of the European Monetary System (EMS), whose function was to be the coordination of the economies of member countries. At the same time, the European Parliament was created, as was the European Commission, the organization's principal executive body, and the Council of Ministers.

The European Union (EU) is certainly the world's largest trading area and contains a significant number of the largest importing and exporting countries in the world. There is a long and well established relationship between the United States and the EU. In fact, most of the American capital flow to Europe has gone to EU countries. One reason, of course, has been the desire of American firms to get inside of the tariff barriers and so protect American export markets. Also important has been the growing prosperity of EU member countries. The highly developed markets in these countries have served to accelerate American capital flow to EU countries, as did the anticipation of a completely unified European market by 1992.

For their part, Europeans have also increased their direct investment in the United States, particularly during the 1980s. A favorable exchange rate in terms of the dollar encouraged such investment by Europeans. The United States also has the largest single market for goods and services in the world. The Europeans have not been as forthcoming to their Eastern and Central European neighbors. The exception, of course, has been the heavy West German investment in the former East Germany.

EMERGING MARKETS: THREAT AND OPPORTUNITY

Many Germans consider competition from low-wage emerging countries as leading to unemployment in the industrial countries. They cite the exploitation of workers in the emerging market countries due to poor and unsafe working conditions as well as low pay. In their view, the industrial countries should take steps to protect against such competition if their workers are to avoid third-world working conditions. In essence, the emerging market countries lose three times as many people as the industrial countries, and they are willing to work for much less in terms of wages and working conditions.

Some idea of the wage gap between the industrialized countries and the emerging market countries is suggested by the fact that German labor costs in manufacturing registered $24.90 per hour per worker in 1995 and in the United States and Japan about $16 to $17 an hour. These figures are in marked contrast to hourly labor costs in Mexico of about $2.40, South Korea $4.90, and less than $2.40 in China. It is no surprise that labor-intensive firms in the developed industrial countries have a significant incentive to move to countries with lower labor costs. Certainly such incentives and concerns are at the center of opposition within the United States to NAFTA as well within the EU to its expansion.

These concerns may be overdrawn. They tend to ignore the fact, for instance, that the productivity of the average American worker is higher than that of the average Mexican. In fact, the labor costs per unit of output between the two workers differ more than their wage differentials alone would suggest. Due to technology, skills, and environmental conditions, American workers can compete with Mexican workers despite receiving higher wages. As Mexico reduces trade and investment barriers and continues with its reforms, new and more modern technology at the disposal of its workers will increase and so will their productivity. The net result will be a rise in Mexican wages rates and/or a rise in Mexico's exchange rate. The fact is that trade opens new opportunities. It is simply incorrect to assume that the world's output is fixed and that any increase in Mexico's output comes at the expense of American output and jobs.

This is little more than a demonstration of the well-established principle of comparative advantage. Accordingly, any country will be better off in terms of jobs, output, and consumption if it specializes in those industries and activities in which it possesses a comparative advantage. The United States, for instance, should concentrate on high-technology industries such as aircraft while importing the goods and services which other countries can make more cheaply. Such an arrangement will assure that the export earnings of emerging market countries will allow them to buy skill-intensive goods from the industrialized countries.

The observation that in recent years living standards in the United States have risen only slowly because of rising imports oversimplifies what is taking place. More to the point is the fact that investment in the United States has been low, producing a slow growth in the country's productivity. Increased trade will serve to benefit all countries—emerging as well as industrial. This does not mean that some groups of workers will not participate in such an increase in prosperity. The losers will likely be those with few, if any, skills.

We learn from our economic theory and the factor-price equalization theorem that trade does indeed effect different workers' wages. From our theorem, we learn that trade will reduce the relative income of the type of labor that is relatively scarce in a country. A case in point: the United States where unskilled labor is relatively scarce and skilled labor relatively abundant, trades with Mexico, where unskilled labor is relatively abundant. In this example, the United States will specialize in skill-intensive industrial products and import the Mexican labor-intensive products. The end result is that the United States will increase its output of skill-intensive industries while Mexico increases its output of those that are labor intensive. The demand for unskilled labor in the United States will decline, and so will U.S. wages relative to those of skilled workers. In Mexico, on the other hand, the wages of unskilled workers will tend to rise.

This is what appears to have taken place as imports from emerging market countries have increased. Thus the wage gap between skilled and unskilled workers in the United States has increased. In fact, such wage differentials have also increased in 12 of the 17 countries of the Organization of Economic Cooperation and Development (OECD) in the 1980s. In some continental European countries, including Greece, Germany, and Sweden, wage differentials remained flat or fell. The reasons apparently are the floor set in these countries by minimum wages, strong trade unions, and generous welfare and other benefits. One consequence has been a fall in the demand for unskilled labor and increased unemployment in these countries.

Not everyone agrees that the globalization of markets is impoverishing low-skill labor in the industrial countries. Some observers note that U.S. trade with low-wage countries, where wages are less than half of those in the United States equals only 3 percent of the GDP. They point out that this is not much higher than the equivalent figure of 2 percent in 1960, when Japan and some European countries were counted as low-wage countries. They would attribute the increasing wage inequality to the technological revolution of the 1980s. In particular, these observers cite the declining demand for unskilled workers to the growth of computers and robots, which can now do the repetitive tasks previously done by such workers.

Undoubtedly, demand in the industrial countries in the future will shift from low-skilled workers in favor of the skilled workers. There is also little doubt that such shifts will increase the mismatch between available jobs and the skills of the unemployed. As a result, we may expect shortages of skilled labor existing alongside significant unemployment of unskilled workers. The quick fix to such a situation is not in trade barriers and subsidies to protect low-skilled industries. Such short-term help that would be provided to low-skilled workers would come at the expense of the rest of the economy. The effect would be to postpone or delay required restructuring in the economy and the creation of fewer jobs.

All this leaves government policy makers with few options that make long-term sense. They can increase the demand for low-skilled workers through such measures as public works programs, job subsidies, and the like. This is likely to be of only short-term benefit. It also raises the question of whether such efforts are the best use of scarce tax resources. They can increase the education and training of workers and so reduce the supply of unskilled workers. The problem is that it may be more effective to focus on new and young entrants into the labor force rather than on middle-aged workers with few working years left in which to repay the investment in training. An example of displaced East German workers comes to mind. In any case, the short-term unemployment problem exists. Still another option for policy makers may be to put in place programs designed to redistribute income and so narrow the gap between the skilled and unskilled workers. In effect, the challenge is how to tax the gainers and compensate the losers without devastating incentives in the process.

Clearly, the challenge to the industrial countries is to search for workable solutions acceptable to gainers and losers in their societies without resorting to trade barriers against emerging market countries. It is in the general interest of workers in the industrial countries that emerging market countries develop as rapidly as possible since the fastest growing markets are to be found in these countries.

A case in point is the registered decline in manufacturing jobs in industrialized countries. Similarly, emerging countries are increasing their share of world manufacturing output. There is, moreover, a shift to service industry jobs from manufacturing jobs within the industrialized countries. Some of the shift may be a statistical artifact due to the way manufacturing jobs are now organized. Thus many of the former in-house service activities in these firms are now farmed out (e.g., accounting, and legal). Another factor that is important in the shift to service industries is in response to a change in consumer demand in these countries. The result is that in the mid-1990s more than half of the output and jobs in industrial countries are in the service industries.

The evidence suggests that governments in the industrial countries should focus their attention on moving more of their citizens into service industries. To facilitate such a transition, governments in these countries should deregulate their markets in services and encourage other countries to do the same. Entry barriers and restrictive practices in service industries tend to be strongly entrenched. These countries should also work to ensure that their citizens are well educated and trained to do the best service sector jobs.

An increasing proportion of service workers are highly skilled, and their skills are based on knowledge. The jobs that demand the best education have been the fastest growing.[3] In the 1980s, the biggest rise in the service sector unemployment was in finance, insurance, property, and business services. In 1987, around 30 percent of Americans in such jobs had a university education compared with just 18 percent in manufacturing.

Moreover, many of the service industries have become increasingly high tech. Firms in the world's increasingly interconnected and complex financial markets need ever more sophisticated computer programs. An example is the rapid growth of worldwide telecommunications and entertainment industries. To this may be added the rapidly growing health-care business, which demands increasingly sophisticated medical and pharmaceutical research.

Policy makers in industrial countries should also realize that employment problems resulting from shifts from manufacturing to service industries may be more apparent than real. For instance, changes in manufacturing and service industries have blurred the distinction between the two. Thus, manufacturers have come to rely on services for a greater proportion of their imports. Cars, computers, and other high-tech goods are not merely manufactured—they are also designed, marketed, advertized, and distributed. A significant and rising part of the value added by manufacturers now consists of services.

In some industrial countries, to the extent that the decline in manufacturing employment is real, their governments should be careful in how they react to pressures to prevent further shrinkage of manufacturing through subsidies or trade protection. The fact is that subsidies and import duties do little or nothing to encourage efficiency in countries' manufacturing industries. Such practices are more likely to do considerable harm due to the diversion of resources away from more productive sectors and the creation of jobs elsewhere in the economy. The end result may be fewer jobs in both the manufacturing and services industries.

It is not surprising that many of the sharpest minds in the emerging market countries are focused on promoting free trade. It is also of considerable concern that those in industrial countries who are most fearful about the future seek to lessen their countries' reliance on the free market economy and have made it their first goal to limit the influence of free trade. For different reasons, both views recognize that a free market economy in a country is ultimately inseparable from its industrial counterpart.

The promising new institution for promoting market economics is the World Trade Organization (WTO), the successor to the General Agreement on Tariffs and Trade (GATT). The new organization offers a powerful mechanism for resolving disputes over trade. Its decisions on trade disputes promise to be much harder to block than under GATT. It has the promise of providing an arrangement whereby arguments over trade are not subject to capture by protectionists. This assumes, of course, that governments will comply with the ruling of WTO. If not, the WTO may soon be defunct.

It is not at all clear that many industrial countries or, for that matter, emerging market countries, will accept the rulings of WTO without protest or worse. In particular, there is danger that the efforts of WTO will be marginalized by the growing enthusiasm for such regional arrangements as we have discussed (i.e., EU, NAFTA, and East Asia). Regional arrangements such as EU can be obstacles to liberalization of trade beyond their borders. Regional free trade pacts can promote global free trade, given that members continue to lower trade barriers against imports from other countries and remain open to all comers willing to join on the same terms.

The defense for regional arrangements of industrial countries rather than broader multilateral arrangements has been the argument that poorer countries are reluctant to embrace freer world trade. This no longer appears correct. It now appears that industrial countries are the ones to raise concerns about open and free markets. It may be that industrial countries now sponsor regional arrangements to limit the growth of freer global trade. The extent to which they will accept the new trade regime encapsulated in WTO remains to be seen.

NOTES

1. See, for instance, Sanjoy Hazarika, "An Indian City of the Future With the Lure of the Past," *The New York Times*, Monday, August 28, 1995, p. C6.

2. See Julia Preston, "Mexico's New Rebel Students Just Want Careers," *The New York Times*, Tuesday, October 3, 1995, p. A3.

3. *The Economist*, March 19, 1994, Vol. 330, No. 7585, pp. 91–92.

10

Changing Nature of Capital Flows:
A Word of Caution

A KEY LESSON: BE CAREFUL

In the past few years, in almost every part of the developing world (including the former socialist countries), reform of economic policy is a key item on the agenda. Closely related is the revival, in new forms, of flows of private capital. Economic reform and private capital together promise a big increase in profitable investment. Optimism in the future of emerging markets may be correct.

Of course, this is not the first time that such optimism was misplaced. Our discussion of the debt crises of the 1970s and 1980s provides examples of more recent history. Economic euphoria soon turned to bitter disappointment, especially in regions such as Latin America, where for more than 10 years countries such as Mexico, Brazil, Argentina, and others took on debts that could only be justified if heroic assumptions about future economic growth and interest rates proved correct. They did not. When dollar interest rates rose in the early 1980s, default by borrowers became reality. Little surprise that creditors collectively turned to save themselves and threatened the world's financial system with collapse.

One way to avoid earlier experience is to focus on improving the quality of foreign investment and not simply on the quantity of such investment, important though it is. This study underscores the reforms underway in the emerging market countries. Macroeconomic and monetary policies have worked to curb chronically high rates of inflation. Fiscal affairs which formerly were little more than a source of instability are now under better control through broadly based tax reforms and rethinking the role of the state in these countries.

These policies have now been reinforced in the emerging market countries by policies designed to open their economies to trade. Many of the emerging market countries have now, in many respects, more open economies than the industrial countries. They have privatized state-owned enterprises; deregulated industry, commerce, and domestic finance; and adopted convertible currencies. In fact, governments that once discouraged inward investors now go to the financial centers of industrial countries to advertise opportunities for foreign investment.

Increasingly, moves away from heavy-handed state intervention toward more liberal economic policies in the emerging market countries have also increased their attractiveness to foreign investors. This also explains in part the change in the pattern of foreign investment flows from earlier periods.

Thus, a far smaller share than in the 1970s and 1980s takes the form of bank lending; bond and equity finance are far more important than earlier, and the volume of foreign direct investment is much greater. These changes underscore the new opportunities created by financial liberalization, privatization, and better prospects of macroeconomic stability. They also serve to strengthen private sector links between the emerging market economies and the international capital markets as well as to encourage governments to hold steady on their reform course.

All this supposes that domestic and international financial systems will continue to work as expected. History suggests that when the financial and monetary systems go wrong, the damage is widespread. While the opportunities for both emerging market countries and industrial countries have increased, so have the risks.

Experience tells us that transition from a tightly controlled domestic financial and monetary system to a substantially unregulated one has proven to be difficult. Even in the well-advanced industrial countries, such reform has been difficult, as indicated by their business cycles in the 1980s. In many emerging market countries, including the former socialist countries, problems of financial reform are made all the more difficult by a large and growing stock of bad domestic debt. Problems become all the more formidable when integration with the outside world is attempted at the same time. In particular, there is greater vulnerability to various kinds of economic shock. Financial and monetary organizations have demonstrated on more than one occasion in history being wrong rather than right. One or two more experiences with emerging markets such as Mexico may be enough to discourage the industrial countries' portfolio investors from all such markets.

History is strewn with many a financial and monetary breakdown. Many came without warning and great did damage, as we have discussed. The principal lesson to investors and governments is to be careful. Complacency in finance invites disaster. This must be remembered when judging and encouraging flows of capital to emerging market countries.

THE ALERT INVESTOR

This study has described at length the new pattern of investment flows to emerging market countries. Unlike the earlier period, when the supply of capital by and large came from banks, a much smaller share now comes from this source. Capital now is directed to private firms rather than governments and/or state-owned firms. Foreign investors are now much more discriminating in favor of selected countries than in the 1970s and 1980s. Finally, the changing pattern of capital flows has also produced changes in risks and incentives for investors and recipients.

The changing pattern of capital flows does not promise much for those countries not so favored. In particular, the world's poorest countries (e.g., sub-Saharan African countries) will likely receive a diminishing share of international capital. These countries have in the past received, and indeed relied on, grants and loans from industrial countries. This is in marked contrast to the experience of the Latin American region, where private capital flows have increased significantly.

Reasons for reluctance on the part of private investors to view Africa with favor owes much to the region's various governments and to the sheer magnitude of problems. Not only are many of the governments inept and corrupt, but the quality of the labor force and poor infrastructure preclude serious private investor consideration. Participation by the international financial community will be required at some point if serious development is to take place. For their part, foreign investors are more cautious than in the past, but their caution will not prevent them from responding to sound investment incentives even in sub-Sahara African countries.

In the 1990s, changes from bank finance to foreign direct investment and capital market finance are striking.[1] In the mid-1980s, the share of private finance in developing countries fell to about 16 percent, due in part to the special circumstances of the debt crisis. By 1991, 30 percent of the developing countries' aggregate capital inflow come from the private sector. Even more significant, the private sector's share of bond finance increased from 4 percent in 1989 to 47 percent in 1992. By and large, the reasons for this transformation are those already maintained. Privatization of state-owned firms is certainly a big reason. To this, of course, may be added the adoption of a broad range of other pro-business policies, including deregulation and lower tariffs and taxes.

For instance, direct foreign investment has long been the largest component of the renewed flow of capital to emerging market countries. This component includes expenditures on acquisition of new firms, intrafirm loans, and retained earnings of foreign-owned firms. What distinguishes direct foreign investment from other components of investment is that management and other intangible assets are also included in the transfer. In short, such investment carries with it investor control. Not surprisingly, governments in developing countries in the past have attempted to avoid or minimize such investment.

The situation has changed so that by 1991, Mexico, China, Malaysia, Argentina, and Thailand accounted for approximately $18 billion of the roughly $40 billion total for world direct foreign investment in developing countries. Much of this growth can be attributed to increased privatization in these emerging market economies. The very act of privatization further encouraged investors to invest in promising projects in these countries. Add economic stability and creditworthiness and emerging market economies, have a promising future.

Even more rapidly growing are portfolio flows of capital into emerging market economies as we have discussed earlier. These flows now increasingly include investment in bonds, equities, and related securities. Reasons for such increases include, on the average, higher returns than in the industrial countries. Of course, returns on the securities in emerging markets are also riskier.

A number of emerging market economies are now enjoying good ratings (investment grade) by the world's main credit rating agencies. Average ratings have improved considerably since the 1980s. Such ratings are important to all portfolio investors. For bond investors, who are promised a fixed rate of return with no participation in the firm, the value of such ratings is paramount. Industrial countries such as the United States have tight institutional rules for investors, particularly those involved in American pension funds. As stated in this study, portfolio investment tends to flow along regional lines, which explains in part the heavy favor given Latin American countries whose credit ratings have improved sharply.

Many of the emerging market countries, moreover, have reduced financial restrictions formerly imposed on foreign investors. Countries such as Argentina, Brazil, Indonesia, and Peru allow foreigners virtually unlimited access to their stock markets. Some countries, including Bangladesh, Chile, Mexico, and others, allow foreign investors fairly free access to listed stocks, although sometimes with restrictions on repatriation. In still other countries (e.g., former socialist countries), stock markets now exist where none did before. Nevertheless, limited information and poor regulatory standards continue to plague these markets, reducing their attractiveness to many foreign investors.

Certainly, emerging market countries have sharply exposed themselves to the volatility of international money and capital markets. These markets are turbulent. Prudent governments in emerging countries should take steps to ensure some security from the turbulence that will surely follow once their economies are fully integrated into world capital and finance markets. After all, forecasting international capital flows is a hazardous business in the best of times, and many a forecaster has been surprised. There is one constant: Equity investors everywhere tend to prefer their own home markets regardless of the location of foreign markets.

Nonetheless, important forces do suggest that emerging market countries are more likely to grow faster than industrial countries in the long term. The share of industrial countries in emerging markets is also likely to grow as a result. Moreover, investors from industrial countries are increasingly aware that returns in emerging markets tend to be weakly correlated with returns in their own stock markets. Cleverly utilized, such a combination would enable investors to strike a better balance between risk and return by moving into emerging markets and constructing a portfolio containing equities in both markets. In essence, the evidence does suggest that opportunities in equities in emerging markets do exist. In the long term, likely returns on investment, as judged by global investors, will carry the greatest weight. On this score there is good evidence that since 1945 it is not the quantity of investment that counts, but the quality.

UNRESOLVED ISSUES

Of course, not all countries or regions will share in the prosperity forecast for emerging markets. A case in point is Egypt and the Arab world.[2] In 1960, the seven leading Arab economies had an average per capita income of about $1,500, while the East Asian countries, including Taiwan, South Korea, Hong Kong, Singapore, Thailand, Malaysia, and Indonesia, had a per capita income of about $1,400. The Arabs were a little ahead. By 1991, however, the per capita income of Arab countries was only about $3,300, while the East Asian countries cited an increase to more than $8,000 per capita.

In 1995, the Arab Middle East attracted about 3 percent of global foreign investment, while East Asia attracted 58 percent. Egypt exported and imported more goods and services in the 1970s than it did in 1995 relative to the size of its economy. In effect, Egypt was more integrated with the world economy in 1970 than it was in 1995.

Egypt and the Arab countries simply are not attractive to foreign investors, as are other countries. By and large, the Arab world has failed to institute the structural reforms that would make it attractive to foreign investors and competition with the rest of the world. It is indicative that Egypt has failed to reform its commercial codes, arbitrary tax regulations, and red-tape foreign investment rules. The situation is so serious that the World Bank estimates that the Arab states and Iran will have to create 47 million new jobs by the year 2010 just to accommodate the population boom that will enter the labor force by then.[3]

Emerging market countries do need the global market for capital. Many of the debt-ridden countries have not fared well in the global market, in good part due to self-inflicted wounds. Circumstances have now changed and many countries have put their financial and economic house in order. Still, problems continue in these countries.

In particular, the conduct of monetary, fiscal, and exchange rate policies in emerging market countries has increased in complexity as a consequence of the types of capital flowing into these countries. It would be unfortunate if in some future breakdown and crisis the blame is placed on free market and political reforms. A case in point is the failure of monetary and financial reforms in a number of Latin American countries in the late 1970s and early 1980s. Even in the 1990s, arguments continue among economists and politicians as to what exactly went wrong in many of these countries.

There are important differences between the world of the 1990s and that of earlier periods. Nonetheless, policy makers should be alert to signals of possible trouble. It will be recalled that a number of the Latin American countries (e.g., Argentina, Chile, and Uruguay), in their reform efforts of their monetary, banking, and financial systems, reduced interest ceilings in domestic rates, allowing their banks greater freedom of action. Many of the controls on capital movements were also reduced in these countries.

The net effect of the reforms in these countries was a sharp rise in their interest rates. These rises proved to be not temporary, but sustained for much longer than expected. The consequent capital inflows promoted by these rises led to the appreciation of exchange rates in the reforming countries and a subsequent deterioration of their trade balances. One consequence of such trade balance deterioration was to encourage Argentina, Uruguay, and Chile to abandon their reform efforts in the early 1980s.

One lesson of the 1970s and 1980s is that emerging market countries in the 1990s should be alert to the exchange rate implication of their reforms. They may have fewer choices in the 1990s world than earlier for the pace of their reforms. It is much more difficult to impose effective controls on capital flows in an increasingly integrated global market. Any rigorous controls that government may impose as simply swimming against the tide of global flows. Many of the controls at best are a nuisance and at worst redirect flows into often illicit channels. In any case, they deprive financial institutions from diversifying their holdings of assets in risk reducing ways. At the same time, controls serve to promote rent-seeking and corruption.

If, in fact, emerging market countries suffer from exchange rate problems because of large capital inflows, economic theory suggests several courses of action, some more desirable than others. The first is, of course, to do nothing. If the exchange rate is fixed, let the rate float. If the capital inflow is of long duration, the exchange rate will have to change eventually. If it is of short duration and temporary, some action can be taken to prevent the exchange rate overshooting and thereby causing problems for exporters. The idea is not to stop the capital inflow, which permits a country to invest more than it saves.

Another well-tried method to deal with rapid capital inflows is for a country to reduce interest rates. The domestic effects, however, may not be desirable. The same conditions that attracted the capital inflow and so promoted an expanding economy may now, by lower interest rates, encourage domestic borrowing, thereby fueling the on-going boom.

Other methods available to emerging countries for controlling inflow and outflow of capital do not yield promising results. These may include sterilization of the capital inflow by selling government bonds. If carried out on a large scale, however, the government will have to raise its own interest rates to make the bonds attractive. This, in turn, will draw in more foreign capital. In due course, the government will have created another problem for itself in the form of an increase in the bill for debt service. Some observers suggest a combination of fiscal policy, partial sterilization by privatizing state-owned enterprises, and moderate appreciation of the exchange rate. In fact, such a combination of measures appears in force in some Latin American countries in the mid-1990s.

Whatever the advantages of such measures for preventing adverse consequences of capital flows for emerging market economies, not all of the emerging market countries are in a position of full control over their fiscal policy, public spending, and tax base. To this may be added the problem of sequencing policies in countries just embarking on economic reform. If a budget deficit is not brought under control, freeing capital flows may not only appreciate the country's exchange rate and so create difficulties for domestic and export industries, but may further enable the government to continue to borrow and prolong the budget deficit. Measures to curb the deficit, always politically unpopular, may be postponed and future fiscal problems made more difficult.

In countries such as the former socialist countries of Europe, where price distortions are severe, liberalization of capital flows may result in simply moving new investment into existing or uneconomic projects. The net effect may be to reduce the country's output. Where domestic prices are so distorted and out of line with world market prices, any new investment will end up producing goods and services that are simply worth less than the resources used in their production. There are exceptions in instances of severely distorted economies (e.g., the establishment of free trade zones, in which producers pay free trade prices for their materials and receive free trade prices for their products). Finally, an inadequate and unstable financial and banking system will make reform a useless exercise and private capital, whatever its source, powerless to promote a country's development.

It is thus that most analysts give banking and financial reforms top priority for emerging market countries and, indeed, for industrial countries as well. These reforms have not always received the attention that they require. They have been forcefully brought forward by the financial and banking difficulties in the leading industrial countries (e.g., the United States, with its savings and loan problems, and Japan, with its huge amount of bad bank debts). They are underscored by the plight of the former socialist countries, where the assets of many state-owned banking systems are worthless. Nonetheless, these former socialist banks continue in many instances to extend credit to loss-making enterprises for fear of causing an economic collapse. Attempts to curb such practices have promoted other practices of enterprises borrowing from each other and leaving their bills unpaid.

Still other countries have resorted to practices not much better than those in the former socialist countries. Their governments have manipulated the banking and financial system by suppressing the price mechanism in the allocation of credit in favor of projects and enterprises that they wished to promote. They have not put the savings of their people to good use by simply not allowing the domestic banking and financial system to channel these savings among competing uses.

Domestic financial and banking systems properly operated serve to enhance a country's savings and effective investment. A proper system, moreover, promotes a country's transformation and merging into global markets. Governments should leave their people in no doubt about the direction of reform. In the case of banking and finance where new skills and institutions need to be created (e.g., former socialist countries), the paradigm of an entirely free market is not always the best solution. Some analysts would tightly restrict the number of a country's banks to restrict competition deliberately and ensure that banks could be profitable. In this way, banks would be given an incentive to be prudent in their lending and so avoid being eliminated and/or merged. No country has thus far come up with satisfactory answers to regulating banking and finance due to the unique problems that they present.

A case in point is that of deposit insurance. Most countries have in place some arrangement to protect depositors from bank failure. The reason is obvious: The fear of banking failure may spread and become a self-fulfilling prophecy. The net effect may be the destruction of the payments system that banks provide and a serious depression, well documented in the histories of countries such as the United States.

At the same time, however, with deposit insurance, bank owners may have little to lose in continuing to operate in a risky manner even in the face of ever-increasing prospects for failure. There is little check on the temptation to lend to less creditworthy borrowers at high interest rates, thus attracting the money a bank needs by paying depositories, in turn, high interest rates. Moreover, if the bank was already on shaky financial grounds, its owners may see less rigid lending practices as a way to restore their fortunes. Something of this sort may be behind the savings and loan problem in the United States. Even competent and sophisticated bank supervision such as exists in the United States and Japan has not been able to control problems in banking. The problems in countries without such sophistication and competence appear overwhelming.

The former socialist countries again provide a good example of the issues at hand. Many borrowers in these countries are doing so simply to pay wages and remain in operation. They are not borrowing in order to invest. Eventually the central authorities acquire the worthless assets of these banks, thereby increasing the size of their debt. The alternative to widespread default is, in effect, to monetize the debt by printing more money. The net result is high and persistent inflation.

The on-going transformation of international finance has implications not only for emerging market economies, but also for industrial economies as well as such international organizations as the IMF and World Bank. For instance, transformation processes may be facilitated by allowing emerging market countries easier access for their firms to markets and listing those firms on the exchanges of industrial countries. Facilitating tax treaties between these countries would also encourage equity investment by avoiding double taxation. In any case, private investors, both domestic and foreign, are to be encouraged to be cautious in their selection of private firms in which to invest. This helps to channel resources to more efficient uses.

NOTES

1. See *The Economist*, September 25, 1995, Vol. 328, No. 7830, pp. 19–20.

2. See Thomas L. Friedman, "Egypt Runs for the Train," *The New York Times*, Wednesday, October 18, 1995, p. A17.

3. Some idea of the magnitude of the problem, including the priorities of the political leadership, is indicated by Thomas Friedman when he writes that in 1994, when 500 Egyptian businessmen gathered for the country's biggest ever economic conference, President Hasni Mubarak canceled his scheduled meeting with the businessmen so that he could receive the President of Mauritania. Ibid., p. 17.

11

Mutual Funds, Banks, and Potential Problems

A POTENTIAL PROBLEM?

Potential problems in the banking and financial organizations in the emerging market countries and industrial countries may not be the only source of concern for investors, savers, and policy makers. Some observers now point with equal concern to the mutual fund industry, so important as a vehicle for investment in emerging country markets.[1]

America's mutual fund industry has grown from just under $500 million in 1985 to more than $2.6 trillion in 1995 as savers have pulled their money from low-yielding bank deposits and other investments. If investors decided in response to rising interest rates to pull out of mutual funds suddenly, the consequences for economic stability may be serious. The redemption of mutual fund holdings could create a vicious spiral of falling assets prices, resulting in worldwide financial and economic distress.

Mutual funds do have several disadvantages. Fund managers are often forced to react to the emotions of the market. Hit with a flurry of redemption requests, they must come up with money and so are forced to sell. This invariably occurs when the market is down, so the fund unloads at the worst possible times. Moreover, when shareholders send in cash, the fund is sometimes forced to buy when prices are high. In addition, managers are often under pressure to take risks in order to achieve short-term results. Of course, many funds carry hidden charges, including management fees and back-end redemption fees. The investor often also pays for advertising and other expenses. So-called no-load funds may include concealed fees.

There is also the issue of the size of many funds and the legal restrictions that constrain them and may hinder their flexibility and speed. A case in point is that they often cannot invest in small-capital stocks. In effect, the funds may do no better than investor direct investment due to the constraints within which they operate.

Not all investors are comfortable with delegating responsibility to someone else to make decisions that affect their money. Individual fund investors may forfeit access to essential information and lose control over key investment decisions.

The alternative, of course, is for individual investors to set up their own portfolio and so become their own manager. Thus they can follow an investment strategy suitable to their own requirements. For instance, an individual may choose to follow a "contrarion" strategy, capitalizing on opportunities to buy when everyone else is selling. This is likely an advantage an individual may not have with a fund.

There is a tendency of various writers in the investment industry to create more confusion than necessary. It is, of course, understandable that financial professionals have an interest in creating an aura of indispensability for their services. There are also individual professionals who insist that anyone can understand the stock market. they argue that the small investor's flexibility and ability to move fast actually provide an edge over the professionals. This may be encouraging to the individual investor who desires to take responsibility for his or her money, decisions, and program and hopes to achieve financial security and care for his or her family's needs, of their families including retirement.

Other advantages for do-it-yourself investors include the elimination of an extra layer of risk to their investment. After all, so the argument goes, individual investors will have to spend time funding and finding and selecting a professional broker, money manager, or financial planner whom they trust. In fact, brokers and other financial advisors are rewarded for the commissions they generate, not for the quality of the recommendations or the service they give their clients. Bad advice, conflicts of interests, and outright fraud do occur with unfortunate regularity. An honest and qualified broker, fund manager, or other advisor is unlikely to understand completely a given individual investor's requirements. To avoid such complications, an individual investor may do better on his or her own.

Nonetheless, the concerns that mutual funds may present a source of instability in financial markets due to the largely discretionary nature of mutual fund investments may be overdrawn. Although mutual funds have grown rapidly, they are still far from being a dominant force in financial markets, including equity markets. Thus, in the United States in 1994, mutual funds held less than 13 percent of the $6 trillion of American firms' shares. In short, they held less than the share of private pension funds and far less than the direct holdings of American householders. Any collapse in the mutual funds markets would certainly damage mutual fund firms, but not the entire market.

At the same time, mutual fund money tends to concentrate in individuals' retirement accounts, which are typically long-term investments. A case in point is the American 401(K) funds, which are unlikely to be withdrawn suddenly from the market. In fact, by some estimates the assets of 401(K) funds were growing at an annual rate of about 15 percent in the mid-1990s. Moreover, 40 percent of mutual funds are held by pension funds. In addition, flows from money into equity funds show little correlation with the total return or the big stock market index. All this suggests that, in fact, the industry may not be dominated by nervous investors.

The events of 1994 financial problems tend to confirm the resolve of mutual fund investors to remain with their funds. Mutual fund investors are well aware (or they should be) that markets rise and fall. One American judge in a 1994 ruling threw out a proposed class-action lawsuit brought by disgruntled investors who lost money in 1994 in the high-risk American Heritage Fund. The judge compared the investors with gamblers who tried to sue a casino after they had lost money playing cards.

Certainly even the best performing mutual funds are risky. The more assets fund-management firms possess, the more they will earn. Not only are returns to their investors likely to be increased, but as a result new investors and new money will be attracted. In their attempts to increase returns, they are also likely to increase the risks for already existing investors far more than they might desire. For instance, in 1994 a number of money market funds were using risky derivatives to try to boost returns. It is also possible that fund managers may be doing extremely well and decide to take less risky ventures. Either strategy may hurt existing investors, whose interests may be best served if their fund managers maximized risk-adjusted returns all the time. In any event, there is little that individual investors may do except participate in so-called closed-end mutual funds, which forces an increase in existing assets rather than attracts new investors and money.

Whether individual investors and/or groups of investors will do as well in increasing their judgeents in financial markets depends on the issue of predictability in financial markets. Economists argue that beating a perfectly efficient market is a contradiction in terms, if in fact this is the intention of investors.

The strongest piece of evidence for the efficient market view is that returns are not correlated with previous returns. In effect, the idea is that today's price cannot predict tomorrow's price. There is no way to beat the market than by getting information faster. Current prices already reflect all the information on a given security that is available. Old information on the security is already discounted. Only unpredictable news can change prices. Since unpredictable news is unpredictable, so price changes are unpredictable—hence the idea encapsulated in the term *random walk*, in which each price change is unaffected by its predecessor and the system has no memory.

Accordingly, investors are best advised to follow a buy-and-hold strategy for securities rather than accepting advice from brokers, including fund managers. If transaction costs are taken into account, the investors are the losers. Some advisors may perform better than others on occasion, in good measure because of the law of averages. After all, somebody is always beating the market some of the time. It is thus not surprising that the efficient market theory has served to promote index funds, in which investors' money is tied simply to the average performance of the stock market.

Fund managers and brokers operating in efficient markets cannot be expected to beat the market consistently. They can earn higher returns only by being lucky and/or taking bigger risks. Studies suggest that the average money manager produces returns that are lower than market averages. In fact, one study reports that mangers running equity portfolios for a couple of hundred American pension funds between 1983 and 1989 underperformed the Standard & Poor (S&P) 500 by an average of 1.3 percent a year, or 2.6 percent if weighted by size.[2] Furthermore, those results are before subtracting managers' fees and of up to 50 basis points.

Even so, some managers and firms do outperform the market even on a risk-adjusted basis and by significant margins. According to probability theory, this is not surprising. That is, in the first year of a study period, half of all managers will outperform the average; in the second year, half of that half will do so; and so on. In short, the expectation is that winners will tend to regress to the mean.

One reason given by some analysts is that success brought in new money much faster than available investment opportunities, prompting some of the top performing managers to leave. In any case, the laws of probability permit some managers consistently to outperform the market through sheer luck. Long-term data (needed to establish consistent outperformance based on skill as well as correct yardsticks) are simply not available.

It may be that outperforming the market is only among other goals that investors may demand of their fund managers and brokers. Risk may be another important goal. On this score, scattered evidence does suggest that brokers and fund managers may do better than investors in identifying and managing risk. The standard definition of the services that an investor can expect of fund managers includes determining the appropriate level of risk, running a portfolio that achieves it, and minimizing tax and transaction costs. In doing so, fund managers and brokers will also improve the workings of the world's capital markets.

One can also hope that in the long term, money managers will perform well in allocating capital to its most productive uses. To this end, efficient markets require active managers to seek information and put it into prices. In the process, they may deliver to their clients after transaction costs less than market returns.

In support of the view that only higher risks will bring higher returns is the theory encapsulated in the so-called capital-asset pricing model. This model undergirds the investment strategies of many managers. Accordingly, prices do include discounts for certain kinds of risk, which alone explains consistently higher returns by some investors. In effect, the more volatile a portfolio of securities, the lower its price for a given expected return. For all practical purposes, current prices reflect all information about a security. Past developments have already been discounted. Only unpredictable news, which is, of course, unpredictable, can change prices—thus the efficient market theory and the view that even price change is unaffected by its predecessor and that the system has no memory. In sum, we are in a random walk down the market.

Not everyone agrees with the efficient market theory and its closely associated capital-asset pricing model. Critics argue that no market is perfectly efficient in handling information. They hold that there are indeed inefficiencies to exploit even in such markets. The activities of traders exploiting an inefficiency cause it to disappear.

A case in point is that new inefficiencies may continue to appear due to the continuing development of new financial instruments. Obviously, it takes time for traders to learn how to price new instruments. Of course, the fast learners beat the slow ones. In effect, new markets are inefficient markets in this view. To this may be added the so-called noise-traders, who deliberately elect not to maximize their expected return. An illustration of such a trader is a central bank purchasing its country's currency in order to support a price and not a profit.

Moreover, traders tend to be a varied group. They tend to reason and interpret differently the information they do receive. In short, they may have different attitudes to risk as well as different time horizons. Traders may receive the same information but react differently. Not all are irrational, but some will be proven wrong. As a result, a market may misprice assets not because of information flow problems but simply because of different ways of reacting to information.

Such expectations have prompted brokerage firms to employ a considerable number of mathematicians to search for market anomalies as well as predict-abilities of markets. These efforts have produced a computer product for nonlinear statistics that seem to work, but not why they work. It is more or less "data mining." Most economists and statisticians are not enthusiastic about such an approach. In their view, theories must start from how people behave and predict the effects, not begin with possibly spurious patterns in the data and induce their causes.

It may be that the computer approach and "data mining" are not a complete waste of time and effort. For instance, in the 1960s a number of fund managers and brokers were convinced that the stock market is not a random walk. It tends to trend in one direction for a considerable length of time. After all, bull markets and bear markets not only exist, but do persist. Something may be causing the market to have memory. The arrival of fast computers capable of handling large quantities of data encourages search for that something.

For assistance in their search they turned to fractal theory. In effect, these analysts considered that financial markets would prove to be fractal. A fractal object is one that occupies more than a certain number of dimensions but does not fill the next number. Fractal theory in financial markets, as interpreted by some analysts, implies that each day's price depends to some extent on yesterday's, so the market is not a random walk. In essence, the market may show self-similarity at different scales. A random process can reveal a pattern after all.

Some analysts turn to chaos theory for assistance. This theory puts forward the idea that simple systems in which there are few causes can still show noisy and apparently random behavior. Both fractal theory and chaos theory suggest that randomness and order can coexist in any given market.

Though fractal theory and chaos theory may have something to say about financial markets, it is difficult if not impossible to use them. Both theories may be useful in describing rather than predicting financial markets. The skeptics underscore their view with the observation that the rules employed by market traders change too fast.

Nonetheless, there are optimists who argue that both theories may be useful. For instance, evidence does suggest that each market tends to stay in a pocket of predictability for some time before moving on. That is, predictability may be possible if one does not attempt to predict during rapid changes in the market. In effect, if one is encountering rapidly changing conditions in a market, it may be advisable to stand aside and wait for more settled conditions.

Many of the successful market traders will readily agree that it is easy to lose money when a market suddenly reverses itself. These traders also lay no claim to an ability to outperform everyone in the market. They judge success by how consistently they are right. Finally, such traders seldom adhere to any one theory, though each may have a favorite insight in their search for consistent market patterns. Clearly, however, there is no assurance that any trader can know what the market will do tomorrow. Neither chaos theory nor fractal theory nor anything else will solve that problem for the trader.

Whatever pattern in the past has proved a reliable guide to current patterns in the market will tend to be taken as better than a simple roll of the dice. A computer program may be useful to search out such patterns, along with detailed data showing every trade for several years in a desired market. It is also helpful given past experience that such a program incorporates some ideas from nonlinear statistical theory. Of course, computer theories, neural networks, technologies, and related ideas are only aids and not substitutes for individual thinking.

One of the more interesting questions raised by market observers is whether the computerization of markets will fragmentize or centralize them.[3] Undoubtedly, large and important traders will play for ever larger stakes, making it very difficult for the small trader to participate. The big players will not stop at attempts to predict markets. They will want to control them. If you are a big enough player in a market for your own moves to influence the market, then you can predict your own next move.[4] Given past experience, the success rate in cornering markets is not notable. More likely, computer programming will lead to diversities in trading strategies in good part because no single program will remain dominant.

It is also likely that these developments will bring in more traders and increase the market's liquidity. Such increases may reduce transactions costs and thereby improve the functioning of the market. As a result, the ability of markets to generate the resources needed for economic growth will increase. Traders do add value, if only because they reduce individuals' transaction costs and minimize by diversification their risk in investing in securities. In the process, traders will also benefit the markets as a whole.

Various theoretical developments about efficient portfolios and their application are made possible by the development of sophisticated computers, as we have noted. Improved financial data enabled traders to develop programs of lesser or greater complexity. Some analysts and traders may have become overconfident in their abilities to predict the market.

It is, nevertheless, the fast-growing mutual funds that are transforming the way individual Americans invest. These funds are now America's largest buyers of common stocks, municipal bonds, and significant amounts of commercial paper and so-called junk bonds. The products of these funds can be differentiated through various combinations of quality, cost, and convenience. For instance, Fidelity capitalizes on performance and service to customers. Vanguard has become an important fund in the United States by selling no-load funds—those for which buyers pay no purchase fee. Some funds may have so many specialists on board that they in effect replicate the Standard & Poor (S&P) Index at great expense.

In any case, logic and some evidence suggest that the mass of mutual fund customers look to convenience, service, and, at the margin, low fees. Still, mutual funds are a business. Assets under management come from sales. Sales are easier if the fund has an image of performance. True, there are funds with good performance but a poor business and the reverse. The essential ingredient in building a fund's business is to produce an acceptable performance over long periods of time and thus enable the fund to gather the assets. As the market becomes more professional and key players have the same information and skill, it is more difficult for any one mutual fund manager to distinguish himself or herself. As technology develops, moreover, the possibilities to profit from any anomalies in the market will diminish.

A ROLE FOR BANKS?

Banks in most countries continue to be big institutions for mobilizing savings. In some industrial countries, this role is being displaced by other institutions, including mutual funds. Banks continue to act as ultimate lenders of last resort, standing as they do between a systemic financial collapse and intervention of the central banks. They continue to carry out the day-to-day operations of a country's payments system. They continue to ensure that the receiver of a payment is confident that he or she is getting "real" money. Because they are of value to society as a whole, banks will always remain viable entities in the economy.

The franchise of banks in many countries continues to be broadened by technology and deregulation. Banks have come forth with such new products as securitized assets and derivatives and have improved the efficiency with which they distribute old ones. For all those reasons, banks as institutions are likely to remain with us, though they have lost aspects of monopoly.

Disintermediation in banking continues. Studies indicate that since World War II in the United States, banks controlled more than half of the financial services industry. By the mid-1990s, their share was down to a quarter and continues to decline as consumers choose to put their resources in other places, including mutual funds. The business of banking will undoubtedly change to include more revenue from fee-based services, such as cash and information management, trading, and derivatives. No doubt profits will exist for those banks and their management, if it is capable of dealing with rapid change.

In fact, since 1990 most large American banks have offered their own mutual funds. European banks have tended to focus on creating a large new market for life insurance and pension products to accommodate rich baby boomers entering middle age. Unlike their American counterparts, European banks can enter the insurance and securities businesses with few constraints. Few insurance or securities firms have the important advantage of name-brand recognition that established European banks possess. Moreover, strict legal restrictions exist that constrain American banks from marketing mutual fund deposits as insured. Mutual fund operation must be kept physically separate from other deposits in American banks. Moreover, such operations also require new skills not always available in a bank.

Given the difficulties of developing new products and building new skills, a number of American banks have selected the purchase course. Thus banks have acquired mutual funds (e.g., Mellon Bank of Pittsburgh's purchase of the Dreyfus mutual fund). Changing technology, customers, and distribution systems have freed banks to reexamine the nature of their business. To some observers, the essence of a bank is its access to information, from which it builds up its relations with customers. If so, anyone with access to such information (e.g., a telephone company) can be a bank. To survive, banks insist that they must be something more than a warehouse for insured loans. They must adapt and offer new products as demand changes—securities, financial management, and financial products that do not carry federal deposit insurance. This is the answer, American bankers argue, to the challenge of disintermediation. In effect, American banks must have more freedom to offer the same products as their competition.

This may not be a complete answer to the disintermediation problem of American banks. For European banks, a tradition of universal banking has left them free to enter many sorts of businesses, including selling insurance and holding large stakes in industrial companies. The development of large banking and securities industries in Europe has occurred. Few European-run banks have been able to seriously challenge these large industries.

Nevertheless, disintermediation is going on in Europe, albeit at a slower pace than in the United States. Fidelity, the strong competitor of American banks, sells its mutual funds to many European countries. In France and Spain, a significant outflow of bank deposits into mutual funds is taking place. Some of the funds, such as Fidelity, Scudder, Stevens, and Clark, plan to use banks' established names or networks. The reason for such tactics is that in Germany, for instance, money market funds are not allowed. In the Netherlands, a mutual fund company, Robeco, sells its products through the branches of local banks.

Due to the difficulties in penetrating European markets, any retail bank within Europe, America, or another country would need to make substantial investment in branches and technology before it could compete with entrenched local competition. Local banks are perfectly willing to resort to political influence and pressure to keep out competition. These difficulties have encouraged banks with global ambitions to resort to acquisitions rather than organic growth when dealing with Europe. These factors have contributed to the relative absence of strong new bank competition and the adoption of new techniques such as securitization. Other reasons also come to mind, such as the fact that different nations have markedly different laws and regulations as well as special local factors. As privatization proceeds in countries such as France, Spain, and Italy, a new class of shareholders may be unwilling to take low returns inherent in bank deposits. In some countries, moreover, the close relationship between banks and industries has turned into disaster (e.g., the Deutsche Bank failure to spot trouble in one of Germany's biggest industrial groups, Metallgesellshaft, and a large property group, Schneider).

Given the nature of European banking, it is not surprising that European banks have lagged behind American and British experience. In both the Untied States and Great Britain, the barriers between commercial and investment banking are disappearing, while in Europe a long tradition in universal banking has ironically served as a barrier to innovation and development in capital markets.

European banks have had all the powers and protection that some American bankers seek. This has not been helpful. They have been protected, as have their inefficiencies. At the same time, the investment banking advantages of American institutions have increased. In financial innovation, specialization, and ability to provide low-cost financial services, American institutions are well ahead of their European competitors.

For all their complaints about restrictions and poor position when compared to their competitors, such as mutual funds, banks possess a considerable advantage in the form of a subsidy that takes the form of deposit insurance. Many people still prefer to hold deposits in banks in the knowledge that such deposits are insured and safe. This is, in effect, a federal government safety net for banks, without which many banks would disappear. Although protecting depositors, deposit insurance may have served to decrease banking discipline. For example, as a bank approaches insolvency and bankers have lost their capital, its owners have little to lose by chancing everything on a last desperate throw of the dice. Most countries, not surprisingly, have now imposed higher capital standards and increased the insurance premiums banks must pay.

NOTES

1. See, for instance, *The Economist*, October 21, 1995, Vol. 337, Number 7937, pp. 75–77.

2. See the discussion in "Investment Management," *The Economist*, November 27, 1993, Vol. 329, No. 7839, pp. 3–30.

3. "A Survey of the Frontiers of Finance," *The Economist*, October 9, 1993, Vol. 329, No. 7838, p. 22.

4. Ibid.

12

Transformation of Money and Capital Markets: A Role for Monetary Policy?

CHANGING NATURE OF MONEY AND CAPITAL MARKETS

Our discussion has underscored the recent developments in financial intermediation. In particular, the increasing importance of domestic and global money and capital markets has, to an important degree, reduced the role of commercial banks as financial intermediaries. In fact, complex linkages among global markets have increased capital mobility to the degree that very large sums of money cross national frontiers every day. These developments have serious implications for monetary policy.

Clearly, if banks now play a smaller role and/or different role in a country's monetary and financial system, the monetary transmission mechanism may be changed. Such changes may lead to situations in which monetary policy impacts differently on economic activity. They may also mean that monetary policy must be implemented in a different manner than in the past. The globalization of money and capital markets may make it more difficult for monetary authorities and central banks to balance domestic policy consideration against international obligations. In fact, the various and on-going changes in global markets may complicate the tasks of monetary authorities and central banks in judging and dealing with systemic risk and financial crises.

As we have stated, the decline in the United States of bank deposits as a share of household assets and the shift of businesses from banks to capital markets to finance investment spending, together with the growth of nonbank intermediaries such as pension funds and mutual funds, insurance companies, and finance companies, have certainly brought singularly important challenges to monetary authorities as well as regulatory agencies. A case in point is the rapid growth of derivatives and increased cross-border equity holdings. Underlying these developments are a number of factors, including greater inflation and interest rate volatility, improvements in information and communications technologies, and the liberalization of various market and capital controls. Many countries still maintain capital controls or restrictions on international investments by banks and institutional investors. Some evidence indicates that portfolios are generally not as internationally diversified as some people believe. In fact, investors still exhibit substantial home-country bias.

Nonetheless, the changing character of banks and their historically key role in the intermediation process has raised the most concern. Banks were heavily regulated to promote financial stability and serve as a fulcrum for monetary policy. It is therefore important to know whether the changing importance of the banking system undercuts the effectiveness of monetary policy or indeed results in a less stable financial system. It is important to know whether these changes are due to the natural evolution of financial markets or to inappropriate financial regulation. Many of the changes that are occurring are doing so in various countries at different speeds.

Some observers in the United States have expressed concern that the possible decrease in the bank reserve base and the increase in the importance of nonbank intermediaries could undercut the Federal Reserve's ability to affect asset prices and nonfinancial activity in the future. Others now question the reliability of monetary aggregates and note that the Federal Reserve should adjust its policy procedures to a more frequent use of a broader range of indicator variables. Still other analysts warn about excessive reliance on either minimal or real interest rates in the policy process, noting that while interest rates may function as information variables, they are not good targets since they do not provide a nominal anchor for policy. In fact, a good number of analysts underscore the necessity for an explicit emphasis on an ultimate goal of price stability to provide discipline to a discretionary approach to monetary policy.

In some countries, such as Germany, that have not experienced significant structural changes in financial markets, monetary targeting is complicated by special factors such as German reunification and foreign capital flows. The long-run demand for M3 (cash plus deposits) in Germany continues to be stable and remains a reliable intermediate target. Institutional differences in monetary and financial structures in various countries may require different conclusions about the choice of specific monetary policy targets and indicators.

In general, there does appear to be a general consensus regarding policy lessons from financial and capital market changes in most years. Thus little support exists to restrain market developments artificially. There is, however, agreement on the need for stronger supervision. Most observers also agree on the importance of central bank credibility and the need for a nominal anchor to guide monetary policy. An exchange rate which requires intervention is a poor substitute in the face of capital mobility, for fundamental changes in economic policy. It is also important that countries reach convergence before pegging exchange rates or adopt a mechanism for allowing timely adjustment in exchange rate parties as convergence occurs.

A ROLE FOR MONETARY POLICY

It is generally agreed that the role of central banks may change as financial and capital markets change. Certainly, central bankers will have their hands full in protecting countries from systemic risk and in constraining inflation.

There is little doubt that what an economy needs is a monetary policy whereby the public knows both that the monetary authority will do its best and that its best is good, to produce outcomes in terms of inflation and output on which the public can rely. The public must believe that inflation will not be allowed to get out of hand. Without overall price stability, it is difficult for firms and households to interpret market price signals correctly. Price stability and monetary confidence are central to financial and capital markets.

Some observers argue that a fixed exchange system promises to enhance domestic credibility only if people believe there is a long-term commitment to the system. Others stress the importance of building financial markets and institutions so that central banks can conduct policy through market-based means. They argue that a central bank must take the lead role in promoting and securing financial and capital markets.

The emerging market economies face three serious threats to establishing price stability and monetary confidence. One is fiscal reform, which is necessary to remove the inflationary force of budget deficits. Second is a privatization program, currency reform, or other means to reduce the inflationary consequences of the monetary overhang. Third is the fact that positive real interest rates must be established to provide incentives for saving and allow credits to be differentiated on the basis of risk.

The central bank can improve the efficiency of the financial intermediation process and promote public confidence through a system of prudential supervision and through active involvement in the development of the payments mechanism. Central banking evolved from commercial banking. One of the basic functions that created the potential value of central banks was their ability to assist the commercial banks in maximizing value added by intermediation, thereby creating wealth. A central bank does this by liquefying illiquid assets of commercial banks or, in certain circumstances, of the financial institutions.

As a result, the service contributed by the central bank has an economic value in the total market system. In essence, the service of enhancing liquidity is what is crucial to commercial banking and is the major element involved in what central banks do.

In the matter of central banks creating inflation, it is clear that when central banks were under a gold standard, the issue of inflation did not come to the fore as a problem. Basically, gold points and a variety of other mechanisms essentially restricted the credit creation of the financial system and regulated (through international gold flows) the extent to which inflation could take hold. However, with contemporary central banking, domestic currencies are accorded value by fiat. It has thus fallen on central banks to preserve the value of the domestic currency directly. There are many ways in which to operate a gold standard without gold. One such system is a monetary rules regime, suggested by Milton Friedman many years ago.

Inflation in the major industrial countries seems to be under control, at least through the mid-1900s. Average inflation in the seven leading industrial countries fell to 2.3 percent in 1994, which is the lowest level in 30 years. This is well below the double-digit rates which many countries experienced in the 1970s and 1980s.

Some observers place the source of these domestic favorable developments in inflation on microeconomic factors, which have raised productivity and so given a boost to economic growth rates consistent with low inflation. Nevertheless, inflation will again surge if there is rapid expansion in the economies under review. Future developments on the inflation front will depend on monetary policies put in place by the authorities in these countries. Again, the changing structure of the world economy and important developments in emerging market economies contribute to overall stability. The role of monetary policy should not be underplayed. The most important determinant of inflation is money and monetary policy.

There is concern that execution of monetary policy, especially in emerging market economies, may over-emphasize the importance of interest rates, financial instruments, and well-functioning financial markets. In early history and less developed markets, where no market for financial assets existed, monetary authorities (including central banks) held regular auctions of the volume of reserves or high-powered money to guide monetary policy. In fact, if relative prices are free to change and act as signals for resource allocation, monetary policy can be effective. The monetary authorities can maintain price stability and so remove the problem of separating general and relative price changes. This, in turn, will reduce the problem of separating temporary and permanent changes in the price level.

INDEPENDENCE FOR CENTRAL BANKERS?

Some observers argue that, in principle, monetary authorities can also maintain price stability either by fixing the exchange rate or by adopting some adaptive or fixed rule for monetary growth. According to these observers, either of these rules will work if the role is consistent with price stability and the public believes that the central bank will follow the rule. These analysts underscore that neither role guarantees success. They note that a fixed exchange rate rule runs the risk that the exchange rate will not be consistent with price stability or, as in the Chilean experience in the 1980s, that the real exchange rate is revalued. Moreover, a monetary rule may have difficulties in promoting price stability if the velocity of money changes, as may happen due, for instance, to a rapidly changing economic environment.

Price stability in the view of many central bankers is difficult to achieve without leaving considerable independence for the central bank. Independence of the central bank may be easier to obtain when the task is narrowly confined to that of price stability. If the central bank has to participate in all sorts of government activities (e.g., in financing budget deficits and in the formulation of other policies), then it becomes difficult for it to target price stability.

Even more important is to depoliticize the money supply process. To this end, constraints must be imposed on the exercise of discretionary policy by a country's monetary authorities.[1] Apart from privatizing the money supply, an objective set of rules or a monetary constitution would serve to constrain these authorities as needed. Monetary stability and thus general economic stability should rest on institutional arrangements rather than be contingent on the personalities of monetary policy makers.

Variable policies affect expectations, and because they can be changed at any time, they can increase uncertainty in the economy. The fact is that people arguing in favor of discretionary authority are not politically realistic. They tend to be overly optimistic—perhaps even naive—regarding the possibility of enlightened management of the economy by popularly elected governments. Evidence suggests that governments often use their power to produce booms just before elections, followed by inflationary busts once all the votes have been counted.

To correct such an uncertain state of affairs, governments must surrender their discretionary power over monetary policy to a country's central bank whose leaders are, presumably, immune from short-term political pressure. Much has been made of the fact that democracies do just that with their judicial systems. In a well-functioning democracy, it is expected that judges will render fair and impartial verdicts, and many believe this model should be followed for monetary matters as well. Research suggests that the more independent is the central bank, the lower is the country's inflation rate over the medium and long terms.

In this view, central bankers should be given some formal independence to make them one of the checks and balances against the accumulation of power by central government.[2] Accordingly, central bankers would need to be like judges, administering, as it were, the "law." In this case, the law would be consistent monetary policy with an aim toward stable prices. One weakness in this view comes from the technical side—namely, how is this economic stability to be achieved, and do the authorities have the technical tools necessary to do their job given the state of economic science? Another weakness is that in democracies, central bankers need to be subject to the same rules of accountability as any other member of government bureaucracy.

This has not prevented the German central bank from calling for full independence for all European central banks as a condition for European monetary union. In its view, central banks should be given full autonomy to pursue the goal of price stability independently of instructions from their governments. Moreover, a future single European central bank must be independent and have price stability as its top priority.

GOALS, INDICATORS, AND TARGETS OF MONETARY POLICY

Consider the term 0 as it is usually understood by economists. Monetary policy deals with objectives, tools, and processes in the regulation of the supply of money. It is argued that monetary policy primarily influences the value and composition of assets. As a result, it is more circuitous than, for example, fiscal policy, which directly influences income and therefore economic activity. A contrary position is that decisions regarding the demand to hold money really involve a decision about whether it is best to hold wealth in this form or in securities or physical assets. Against such a background, asset holding may be as significant as income in directly influencing economic activity. Monetary policy, through its effect on assets, may theoretically have as direct an impact on economic activity as fiscal policy operating through income.[3]

Monetarists, or quantity theorists, who emphasize the important role of money in economic activity, argue that the monetary authority can control nominal quantities of its own liabilities. By manipulating these quantities, it can fix the exchange rate, the nominal level of income, and the nominal quantity of money. It can also directly influence the rate of inflation or deflation, the rate of growth or decline in nominal national income. The monetary authority cannot, through control of nominal quantities, fix real quantities such as the real interest rate, the rate of unemployment, the level of real national income, and the real quantity of money; nor can it fix the rate of growth of those quantities.[4]

Economists are quick to point out, however, that this does not mean that monetary policy does not have important effects on these real magnitudes. When money gets out of order, repercussions are felt throughout the economy. Monetary history provides ample evidence of this. In fact, the long debate among economists and monetarists—led by Milton Friedman and the Keynesians—over the effectiveness of the use of governmental monetary and fiscal policies to influence economic activity provides us with a valuable example. Keynesians have argued that money and monetary policy have little or no impact on income and unemployment, particularly during some economic depressions. Moreover, government spending and taxation (i.e., fiscal policy) are most effective when dealing with inflation and unemployment problems. Monetarists, including Friedman, have stressed the importance of money. They have argued that a rule requiring the monetary authority to cause the nominal stock of money to increase by a fixed percentage annually would effectively reduce fluctuation in prices, real output, and unemployment.

It is thus generally agreed that by goals of monetary policy we mean ultimate aims and objectives—that is, price stability, economic growth, full or maximum employment, and balance of payments equilibrium. These objectives are shared by most countries.

When viewed individually, each of these goals appears straightforward. It is another matter, however, to achieve all of these goals at the same time. Conflicts arise. Reaching one goal may not make it impossible to reach another. Thus, the closer an economy is to full (or maximum) employment, the faster prices will rise.

Under a system of fixed exchange rates, the balance-of-payments equilibrium requires that the domestic economy be systematically inflated and deflated. Moreover, the goal of economic growth may conflict with any or all of these other goals. It is useful, therefore, to distinguish between a necessary conflict and a policy conflict.

A necessary conflict means that the achievement of one goal necessarily means that another will not be achieved. An example of this is suggested by past arguments over the Phillips curve analysis, whereby a presumed trade-off occurs between full employment and price stability. An example of a policy conflict occurs when monetary policy cannot pursue both price stability and economic growth at the same time. Evidence suggests that a given rate of economic growth is consistent with a given rate of price increase. Countries have also experienced potential conflicts. Thus, except for price stability, monetarists argue that the achievement of other goals by monetary policy manipulation is an illusion.

INDICATORS AND GOALS OF MONETARY POLICY

Given the goals of monetary policy, it is necessary to design a strategy for their achievement. In essence, monetary policy strategy, with explicit goals or objectives, intermediate targets, and operating targets, must be available to the monetary authority. For the success of any given monetary strategy, the monetary authority must have policy instruments to operate targets that, in turn, affect the intermediate targets that change the ultimate goal variables. At the same time, a useful monetary strategy must also have a method to monitor its effects on the economy.

Intermediate targets include monetary aggregates, credit aggregates, and capital market interest rates. Operating targets consist of such variables as bank reserve aggregates, money market conditions (indicated by the Treasury bill rate), free reserves, and, in the United States, the federal funds rate.

The monetary authorities cannot manipulate the money supply as directly as tax rates; nor can they determine the full structure of interest rates. As a result, they must often choose a particular operating target that is easier to manipulate with the instruments available but whose relationship to a particular intermediate target is reasonably well observed. Ready examples are the monetary base (i.e., currency plus the banking system's total reserves) in Switzerland and Italy. Short-term money market interest rates are traditional operating targets in the Untied Kingdom and Austria. In the past, total bank credit has been preferred as an operating target in France. In Germany, some ratio of bank liquidity has been used. In the Netherlands and Spain, their ratio has usually meant the difference between some compulsory ratio of assets to liabilities and the actual ratio.

In essence, the distinction between the operating and intermediate targets varies from country to country. The choice of operating target depends mainly on the monetary instruments available to a country's monetary authorities. The distinction between instruments and targets may be very narrow. For example, the central bank discount rate is an instrument, whereas short-term interest rates as a whole are an operating target. Moreover, the instruments depend on the country's financial structure.

There are at least six categories of instruments that are important. One is central bank transactions in securities. If a well-developed money and capital system exists, central banks can influence interest rates by buying and selling securities (usually government securities). These open market operations must be legitimate. They conflict, however, with a central bank's efforts on behalf of debt management operations for the government.

The second category is a central bank's lending operation. The way central bank lending operates depends on the country and the level of commercial bank indebtedness. In the United Kingdom, for instance, the central bank does not lend directly to commercial banks. It carries on its operations with the discount houses. In other countries, the level of commercial bank indebtedness tends to be high—in France, for example. In any case, a central bank, in its capacity as lender of lost resort, has a special role to play.

The third category of instruments concerns changes in minimum reserve requirements. Again, differences exist among countries. Reserve requirements may be fixed against all deposits or only against special kinds of deposits, as in Switzerland. Some central banks, such as the Geneva and the French, have tended in the past to make frequent changes in reserve requirements. The fourth category is controls in bank lending. Many countries use direct controls in some form. The fifth category is direct control over interest rates. There is a trend toward eliminating such controls in most industrial countries and some emerging market countries, as we have noted. Nevertheless, banks still tend to interpret changes in the discount rate as a signal to change their own rates.

The final category is controls on the foreign transactions of banks in response to foreign exchange movements. These controls are, in essence, manifestations of the aforementioned categories. More straightforward controls prohibit certain classes of transactions abroad or create special exchange rates for such transactions.

Many economists, especially monetarists, have a preference for a monetary aggregate target rather than a money market target as the appropriate target for monetary policy because it is closely associated with their view of the control of universal and real rates of interest. Thus, monetarists hold that the authorities are best able to fix the nominal rate of interest. Their theory on the real rate of interest emphasizes the importance of the link between the nominal market rate of interest and the real rate of interest. Only if the expected rate of inflation is zero will nominal and real rates of interest be equal.

Furthermore, the choice in selecting a monetary aggregate target or money market target is conditioned on the relative importance of random disturbances occurring from the real and monetary sides of the economy. If the real side of the economy is more unstable, then a money aggregate target is preferable. If the monetary side of the economy is more unstable, then an interest rate target is preferred. However, the rate of interest relevant to expenditure decisions, and therefore the position of the IS curve (in the IS-LM curve [Investment and

Savings-Liquidity Money] for a closed economy), is the real rate of interest, which the authorities cannot fix in any case.

The choice of an indicator that will quickly and accurately give the direction and magnitude of monetary policy is also closely associated with the monetarist preference for a monetary aggregate target. A useful indicator must possess such characteristics at a high degree of correlation with the target variables; accurate and reliable statistics on the indicator must be quickly available to authorities; and the indicator should be capable of controlling the variables. Anna J. Schwartz eliminated the distinction between targets and indicators.[5] The ideal target, Schwartz has argued, ought to be judged on three criteria: (1) Is it measurable? (2) Is it subject to control by central banks? (3) is it a reliable indicator of monetary conditions? On the basis of data for the Untied Kingdom, Canada, and Japan, Schwartz concluded that the money stock is the best "target indicator." A similar conclusion has been reached in other studies.

The money supply and its sensitivity to interest rates in several countries have been studied.[6] There is now considerable evidence on the interest sensitivity of some reserve multipliers. If these multipliers are highly sensitive to interest rate changes, then it may be difficult to implement monetary control through the control of reserve aggregates; but to judge from the evidence so far, the interest rate sensitivity of various multipliers is low. Accordingly, control of monetary aggregates through reserves does not present a serious problem.

Alternative approaches to monetary control are not always satisfactory. Thus criticism of Alan Greenspan, Chairman of the Federal Reserve Board of Governors, for trying to fine-tune the American economy in the late 1980s and early 1990s was probably misdirected. It would have been better to have criticized Congress for failing to provide a clear objective for the Federal Reserve, instead of the dual targets of full employment and price stability. The lack of a clear objective probably forced Greenspan to try to fine-tune the economy in order to survive politically during the recession years of that period.

The Federal Reserve contributes to its own problems by insisting on secrecy about what actually goes on in Open Market Committee meetings. The financial market often experiences short-term instability because of this secrecy and because the public is forced to guess about what the Federal Reserve is up to in its activities. In contrast, the world's other central banks typically hold a press conference about their actions, leaving little room for doubt and speculation.

It is certainly correct that during recent years, the Federal Reserve has paid little attention to monetary aggregates, concentrating instead on real variables and on financial indicators, such as the exchange rate on the shape of the yield curve, to steer interest rate policy.[7] Some economists have focused on the Federal Reserve's M2 (currency + demand + time deposits) measure of the money supply to gauge monetary events, but this largely reflects transactions and excludes large time deposits and money market securities. Other economists view the M2 as a leading indicator of the nominal gross national product (GNP). A slump in the M2 is interpreted as a forecast of a slump in general economic activity.

Critics are quick to point out that there is little reason to believe that money figures are better guides to economic activity currently than in the past. In their view, this is little more than the revival of monetarism, which fell out of favor because the various monetary indicators gave misleading readings about movements in the GNP.

The criticism is misplaced. Monetarism does not mean that changes in the money supply *automatically* cause changes in the nominal GNP. Rather, monetarists argue that while the links between changes in money and changes in economic activity are there, their lengths are anything but constant. Therefore, it is futile to try to fine-tune monetary policy by discretionary means, and it is vitally important to have a monetary rule.

Too many critics of monetarism act as though some monetary measure is the fixed point of monetarism. The fact is that one cannot so simply dismiss the principal proposition of monetarism: Increases in the growth of the money supply will increase inflation in the long run and will have no lasting effect on economic activity. It is inappropriate to judge money's relevance by attempting to explain short-run outcomes by long-run relationships.

Evidence reported by G. P. Dwyer, Jr., and R. W. Hafer in their study of several countries is consistent with these relationships. From 1970 to 1984, the relationship between money growth and nominal income in 62 countries was very close. There was little systemic relationship between money growth and real income, and there was a one-for-one correlation between money growth and inflation. Moreover, for the period 1981–1986, evidence from 40 countries supported the same conclusions.[8]

NOTES

1. See George Macesich, *Monetary Policy and Politics: Rules versus Discretion* (Westport, CT: Praeger Publishers, 1992).

2. See "As Independent as Judges," *The Economist*, (April 20, 1991), pp. 17–18.

3. For a discussion of supporting empirical evidence, see George Macesich and Hui-Liang Tsai, *Money in Economic Systems* (New York: Praeger Publishers, 1982).

4. See Milton Friedman, "The Role of Monetary Policy," *American Economic Review*, Vol. 58 (March 1968), pp. 1–17.

5. Anna J. Schwartz, "Short-Term Targets of Three Central Banks," in *Targets and Indicators of Monetary Policy*, Karl Brunner (ed.) (San Francisco: Chandler, 1969).

6. See Macesich and Tsai, *Money in Economic Systems*, pp. 85–133.

7. "Monetarism: Back from the Dead?" *The Economist*, February 16, 1991, p. 62.

8. G. P. Dwyer, Jr. and R. W. Hafer, "Is Money Irrelevant?" *Review*, Federal Reserve Bank of St. Louis (May/June 1988), pp. 3–17.

Bibliography

"Africa: A Flicker of Light." *The Economist*, Vol. 330, No. 7853, p. 24.

Ambirajan, S. "Economics and Economists in the Formation of a Monetary Policy for India, 1973–1893." *History of Political Economy* Vol. 9, No. 1, Spring 1977, pp. 122–143.

Arkoun, Mohammed. *Common Questions, Uncommon Answers*. Trans. and ed. Robert D. Lee. Boulder, CO: Westview Press, 1994.

"As Independent as Judges." *The Economist*, Vol. 330, No. 7201, pp. 17–18.

"Asia's Competing Capitalisms." *The Economist*, Vol. 335, No. 7920, pp. 16–17.

Brooke, James. "Colombia Marvels at Drug Kingpin: A Chain-Saw Killer, Too?" *The New York Times*, Wednesday, June 21, 1995, p. A7.

Brooke, James. "GTE Role in Venezuela Is Warning on Privatization." *The New York Times*, Wednesday, June 21, 1995, p. C1.

Brooke, James. "More Open Latin Borders Mirror an Opening of Markets." *The New York Times*, Tuesday, July 4, 1995, p. C29.

Canzoneri, Matthew B. "Exchange-Intervention Policy in a Multiple Country World." *Journal of International Economics*, Vol. 15, November 1982, pp. 267–89.

Carroda-Bravo, F. *The Mexican Economy*. Boulder, CO: Westview Press, 1982.

Carroda-Bravo, F. *Oil, Money, and the Mexican Economy*. Boulder, CO: Westview Press, 1982.

Centron, Marvin, and Owen Davies. *Crystal Globe: The Haves and Have-Nots of the New World Order*. New York: St. Martin's Press, 1992, Chapter 11.

Cline, William. "Managing International Debt: How One Big Battle Was Won." *The Economist*, Vol. 334, No. 7902, pp. 17–19.

Congress of the U.S. Joint Economic Committee. Japan's Economic Challenge. Washington, DC: U.S. Government Printing Office, 1991.

Daley, Suzanne. "In South Africa a Culture of Resistance Dies Hard." *The New York Times*, Wednesday, July 19, 1995, p. A3.

de la Dehesa, Guillermo. "The Recent Surge in Private Capital Flows to Developing Countries: Is it Sustainable?" Per Jacobsson Lecture, October 2, 1994, Madrid, Spain. Washington, DC: Per Jacobsson Foundation, International Monetary Fund, 1994, pp. 4–5.

De Palma, Anthony. "Telmex Gains in Attempt to Buy Cable-System Stake." *The New York Times*, June 22, 1995, p. C4.

Dwyer, G. P., Jr., and R. W. Hafer. "Is Money Irrelevant?" *Review*, Federal Reserve Bank of St. Louis, May/June 1988, pp. 3–17.

"Democracy in Eastern Europe." *The Economist*, Vol. 332, No. 7630, pp. 52–53.

The Economist, Vol. 328, No. 7830, pp. 19–20.

The Economist, Vol. 330, No. 7852, p. 84.

The Economist, Vol. 330, No. 7585, pp. 91–92.

The Economist, Vol. 333, No. 7891, pp. 42–43.

The Economist, Vol. 334, No. 7906, p. 73.

The Economist, Vol. 335, No. 7911, p. 108.

The Economist, Vol. 337, No. 7937, pp. 75–77.

Edwards, Corwin. "The Dissolution of Zaibatsu Continues." *Pacific Affairs*, September, 1946, pp. 8–24.

Epstein, Gene. Interview with Milton Friedman in *Barron's*, September 4, 1995, p. 41.

Epstein, Gene. "Public Enemy No. 1? To a Nobel Laureate, It's Big Government, Not Budget Gaps" (interview with Milton Friedman). *Barron's*, September 4, 1995, p. 41.

Figes, Orlando. "Without a Fight." *New York Times Book Review*, September 3, 1995, p. 7.

French, Howard W. "French President Affirms Ties to Africa." *The New York Times*, Saturday, July 22, 1995, p. 5.

French, Howard W. "Out of South Africa, Progress." *The New York Times*, Thursday, July 6, 1995, pp. C1 and C5.

French, Howard W. "West Africans Find Prosperity Is Elusive: Region Seems Unable to Overcome Past." *The New York Times*, Sunday, April 9, 1995, p. A9.

Friedman, Milton. "The Case for Flexible Exchange Rates." *Essays in Positive Economics*, Milton Friedman (ed.). Chicago: University of Chicago Press, 1953, pp. 157–203.

Friedman, Milton. "Comments on the Critics." *Journal of Political Economy*, Vol. 80, September–October, 1972, pp. 932–41.

Friedman, Milton. "Economists and Economic Policy." *Economic Inquiry*, Vol. 24, January, 1986, pp. 1–10.

Friedman, Milton. "Free-Floating Anxiety." *National Review*, Vol. XLVI, No. 17, September 12, 1994, pp. 32–36.

Friedman, Milton. "M1's Hot Streak Gave Keynesians a Bad Idea." *Wall Street Journal*, September 18, 1986, p. 32.

Friedman, Milton. "The Role of Monetary Policy." *American Economic Review*, Vol 58, March 1968, pp. 1–17.

Friedman, Milton, and Anna J. Schwartz. *Monetary History of the United States, 1867–1960*. Princeton, NJ: Princeton University Press for the National Bureau of Research, 1963, Chapter 3.

Friedman, Thomas L. "Egypt Runs for the Train." *The New York Times*, Wednesday, October 18, 1995, p. A17.

Gargan, Edward A. "For U.S. Business, a Hard Road to Vietnam." *The New York Times*, Friday, July 14, 1995, pp. C1 and C5.

Gewirtz, Carl. "Gambit for Third World Debt Burden: Baker's Plan Linked to Experts." *International Herald Tribune*, June 21, 1989, pp. 11 and 15.

Golden, Tim. "Mexico Judge in Union Case Is Shot Dead." *The New York Times*, Wednesday, June 21, 1995, p. A7.

Haberler, Gottfried. "Integration and Growth of the World Economy in Historical Perspective." *American Economic Review*, Vol. 54, March 1964, pp. 1–22.

Hazarika, Sanjoy. "An Indian City of the Future with the Lure of the Past." *The New York Times,* Monday, August 28, 1995, p. C6.

"Investment Management." *The Economist,* Vol. 329, No. 7839, pp. 3–30.

Ishihara, Shintaro. *The Japan That Can Say No: Why Japan Will Be First Among Equals.* New York: Simon & Schuster, 1991.

Johnson, Harry. "The Nobel Milton." *The Economist,* Vol. 23, p. 95.

"Kenya: Into the Ark." *The Economist,* Vol. 335, No. 7920, p. 40.

Keynes, John Maynard. *The General Theory of Employment, Interest, and Money.* New York: Harcourt, Brace and World, First Harbinger Edition, 1964, p. 383.

Kindleberger, Charles P. "The Case for Fixed Exchange Rates." *The International Adjustment Mechanism.* Boston: Federal Reserve Bank of Boston, 1970.

Lewis, Paul. "A New World Bank: Consultant to Third World Investors." *The New York Times,* April 27, 1995, p. CA.

Loomy, Robert E. *Development Alternatives for Mexico.* New York: Praeger, 1982.

Macesich, George. *Economic Materialism and Stability.* New York: Praeger, 1985, pp. 1–20.

Macesich, George. *Integration and Stability: A Monetary View.* Westport, CT: Greenwood Press, 1995.

Macesich, George. *Monetary Policy and Politics: Rules versus Discretion.* Westport, CT: Praeger, 1992.

Macesich, George. *Monetary Reform and Cooperation Theory.* New York: Praeger, 1989, pp. 57–64.

Macesich, George. *Reform and Market Democracy.* New York: Praeger, 1991.

Macesich, George. *World Banking and Finance: Cooperation versus Conflict.* New York: Praeger, 1984.

Macesich, George. *World Debt and Stability.* New York: Praeger, 1991.

Macesich, George, and Hui-Liang Tsai. *Money in Economic Systems.* New York: Praeger, 1982.

Maddison, Angus. *The Political Economy of Poverty, Equity, and Growth: Brazil and Mexico.* Oxford: Oxford University Press, 1992.

Marx, Karl. *Das Kapital.* New York: Modern Library, Inc., 1906.

Milapidus, Ira. "Islam without Militance." *New York Times Book Review,* August 21, 1994, pp. 9–10.

"Monetarism: Back from the Dead?" *The Economist,* February 16, 1991, p. 62.

Offe, Claus. "Strong Causes, Weak Cures." *East European Constitutional Review,* Vol. I, No. 1, Spring 1992, pp. 21–23.

Preston, Julia. "Mexico's New Rebel Students Just Want Careers." *The New York Times,* Tuesday, October 3, 1995, p. A3.

Pryce-Jones, David. *The Strange Death of the Soviet Empire.* New York: Henry Holt and Company, 1995.

Puhovski, Z., I. Prpić, and D. Vojnić (eds.). *Politics and Economics of Transition.* Zagreb: Informator, 1993.

Rohatyn, Felix. "World Capital: The Need and the Risks." *New York Review of Books,* July 14, 1994, pp. 48–53.

Rosenthal, A. M. "Taking Over Mexico." *The New York Times,* February 24, 1995, p. A15.

Sanger, Dave E. "At the End, U.S. Blunted Its Big Stick." *The New York Times,* Friday, June 30, 1995, p. C5.

Schatz, Sayre P. *Nigerian Capitalism.* Berkeley: University of California Press, 1977.

Schnitzer, Martin C. *Comparative Economic Systems*. 6th ed. Cincinnati, OH: South-Western Publishing Co., 1994, pp. 73–76, 124–31.

Schwartz, Anna J. "Short-Term Targets of Three Central Banks." *Targets and Indicators of Monetary Policy*, Karl Brunner (ed). San Francisco: Chandler, 1969.

Shuy and WuDunn. "Japanese Do Buy American: By Mail and a Lot Cheaper." *The New York Times*, Monday, July 3, 1995, p. A1.

Simon, David D. *Cities, Capital and Development: The African Experience*. Lymington, England: Belhaven Press, 1992.

Sims, Calvin. "Growls from Military Echo in Peru and Chile." *The New York Times*, Tuesday, June 20, 1995, p. A5.

Singer, H. W., and S. Sharma (eds.). *Economic Development and World Debt*. London: The Macmillan Press, Ltd., 1989.

Smith, Patrick. "The Irresponsible Super Power." *The New York Times*, Saturday, July 1, 1995, p. A15.

"The Struggle for Vietnam's Soul." *The Economist*, Vol. 335, No. 7920, pp. 33–34.

"Surfing through the Languages." *The Economist*, Vol. 335, No. 7920, p. 38.

"A Survey of the Frontiers of Finance." *The Economist*, Vol. 329, No. 7838, pp. 22.

Tavalas, George S. "Some Further Observations on the Monetary Economics of Chicago-ans and Non-Chicagoans." *Southern Economic Journal*, Vol. 42, April 1976, pp. 685–92.

Tavalas, George S. "Some Initial Formulations of the Monetary Growth Rate Rule." *History of Political Economy* Vol. 9 No. 4, Winter 1977, pp. 535–47.

Toland, John. *The Rising Sun: The Decline and Fall of the Japanese Empire, 1936–1945*. New York: Random House, 1970, pp. 5ff.

Turner, Charles. *Japan's Dynamic Efficiency With Global Economy*. Boulder, CO: Westview Press, 1991.

United Nations. *Human Development Report 1992*. New York: Oxford University Press, 1992.

United Nations. *Maldevelopment of a Global Failure*. New York: United Nations Publications, 1990.

Williams, Gavin. *Nigeria: Economy and Society*. London: Rex Collings, 1976.

"Winning Back Their Land." *The Economist*, Vol. 335, No. 7920, pp. 37–38.

World Bank. *Africa's Adjustment and Growth in the 1980s*. New York: Oxford University Press, 1989.

World Bank. *Development Report*. Washington: World Bank, 1983.

Index

About the Author

GEORGE MACESICH is Professor of Economics and the Director of the Institute for Comparative Policy Studies at Florida State University. Dr. Macesich is the author of many books including *Integration and Stabilization* (Praeger, in press), *Monetary Reform in Former Socialist Economies* (Praeger, 1994), and *Successor States and Cooperation Theory: A Model for Eastern Europe* (Praeger, 1994).

ISBN 0-275-95518-4

EAN

9 780275 955182

HARDCOVER BAR CODE